PRAI

Writer for

spells out exactly what you need to do

reach your writing goals this year, I'd be very surprised.

LINDA FORMICHELLI, co-author of *The Renegade Writer: A Totally Unconventional Guide to Freelance Writing Success*

The words "total professional" seem to have been invented to describe Kelly James-Enger. I have been a long-time fan of her previous writing books and I will also highly recommend *Writer for Hire*. This may be the champion of all the writing books James-Enger has written because it contains her best advice compressed into short chapters that make for speedy reads. If you are a service writer looking for the secrets to success, they are all in here! It's taken James-Enger fifteen years of hard-wrought effort to learn them, and now they can be yours. Read closely. Bring a highlighter. Apply what you learn. You'll be so glad you did.

CHRISTINA KATZ, author of *The Writer's Workout, Get Known Before the Book Deal,* and *Writer Mama*

Whether you're a beginning freelance writer or a veteran, *Writer for Hire* is extraordinarily helpful, and a compelling read. You'll find a formula for sure-fire query letters, how to break into business writing or ghosting books, and much more sensible, tested advice. This book brims with serious, step-by-step ways to boost your income, your productivity, and your spirits!

SALLEY SHANNON, President, American Society of Journalists & Authors (ASJA)

If you want to start, refine, or redefine your writing career the right way, pick up this truly foundational book. Chock full of so much solid, sensible, practical and creative advice, information and ideas, this "writing-career compass" will give you an edge right out of the gate.

PETER BOWERMAN, Author, *The Well-Fed Writer* books
www.wellfedwriter.com

As usual, author Kelly James-Enger uses the lessons she's learned from her own incredibly successful freelancing career to provide smart, generous advice written in an easy-to-like style to other writers who need just this targeted nudge to get their own freelance businesses off the ground.

JENNIE PHIPPS, Editor & Publisher, *Freelance Success*

Chock full of practical tips, tools, and gems of wisdom, *Writer for Hire* is the go-to guide for anyone seeking to establish or improve a freelance writing career. James-Enger's companionable voice leads you through the murky world of freelancing and gives you sound advice on all aspects of a writer's business and a writer's life. *Writer for Hire* is a quick, easy read so packed with advice that you'll find yourself reaching for it over and over in the years to come. Whether you're new to the world of freelancing or need a boost to get you back on track, *Writer for Hire* will show you the way.

KELLY L. STONE, author of *Time to Write: No Excuses, No Distractions, No More Blank Pages* and *Thinking Write: The Secret to Freeing Your Creative Mind*

Air Lines
WRITER FOR HIRE

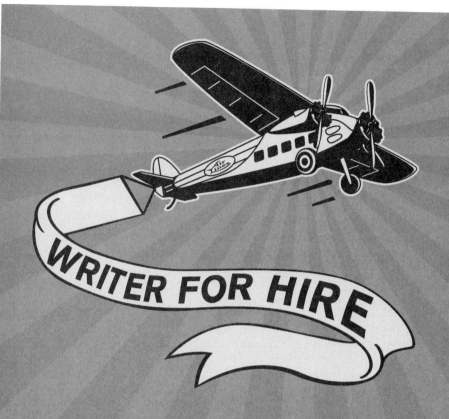

WRITER FOR HIRE

101 SECRETS TO FREELANCE SUCCESS

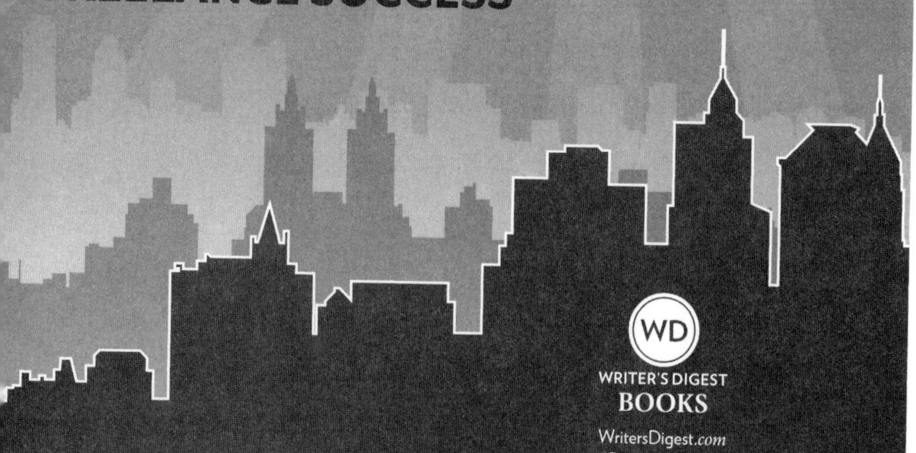

WD
WRITER'S DIGEST
BOOKS
WritersDigest.com
Cincinnati, Ohio

Kelly James-Enger

 Published by Writer's Digest Books, an imprint of F+W Media, Inc., 10150 Carver Road, Blue Ash, Ohio 45242. (800) 289-0963. First edition.

For more resources for writers, visit www.writersdigest.com/books.

To receive a free weekly e-mail newsletter delivering tips and updates about writing and about Writer's Digest products, register directly at www.writersdigest.com/enews.

15 14 13 12 5 4 3 2 1

Distributed in Canada by Fraser Direct
100 Armstrong Avenue
Georgetown, Ontario, Canada L7G 5S4
Tel: (905) 877-4411

Distributed in the U.K. and Europe by F&W Media International
Brunel House, Newton Abbot, Devon, TQ12 4PU, England
Tel: (+44) 1626-323200, Fax: (+44) 1626-323319
E-mail: postmaster@davidandcharles.co.uk

Distributed in Australia by Capricorn Link
P.O. Box 704, Windsor, NSW 2756 Australia
Tel: (02) 4577-3555

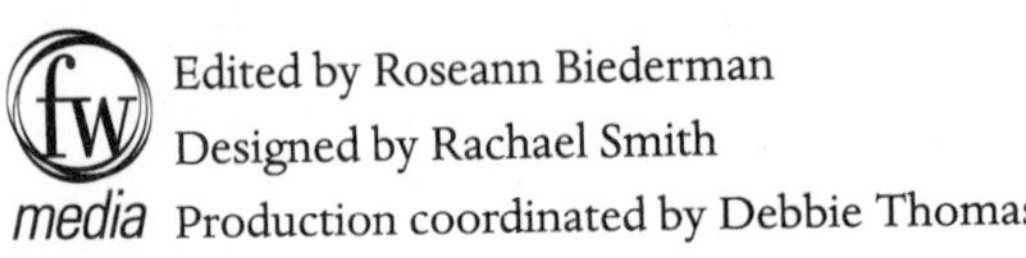

Edited by Roseann Biederman
Designed by Rachael Smith
Production coordinated by Debbie Thomas

DEDICATION

To Ryan and Haley, my two favorite reasons to freelance.

ACKNOWLEDGMENTS

No writer works in a vacuum, and that's even more true for freelancers. I'd first like to thank Jane Friedman for her immediate interest in this book (and to Christina Katz for helping connect us!) as well as Kelly Messerly at Writer's Digest Books and my editor, Melissa Wuske. I've wanted to work with Writer's Digest for years and am thrilled to have become one of its authors.

I'd also like to thank the many freelancers who lent their expertise to this book, including Christina, John Borchardt, Jane Boursaw, Peter Bowerman, Sage Cohen, Meagan Francis, Susan Johnston, Kristen Lambert, Kristin Baird Rattini, Gretchen Roberts, Tina Tessina, and Russell Wild. Extra thanks to my long-term buddies who have helped me negotiate the ups and downs of my career and life, especially Kris, Polly, Sharon, Sam, Hannelore, Jill, Abby, and all three Katies.

Then there are the people who make my work possible: Diana, my favorite child wrangler; my awesome research assistant, Alyssa; and backup babysitters Emma, Grace, and Natalie. Special thanks to Chaleigh for her proofreading services, too.

I thank my mom, who always encouraged my love of reading and writing, and Erik, who supported my desire to freelance from day one even when it seemed liked a crazy idea. While I love freelancing, my favorite role will always be the one of mom, so my most heartfelt thank-you is to Jodi and Chaleigh for making that happen.

Finally, thanks to my readers. I hope this book will help you pursue your freelance dreams and that the reality is even better than you expected.

TABLE OF CONTENTS

PART 4
MANAGEMENT: RUNNING YOUR BUSINESS LIKE A BUSINESS

PART 5
BALANCE: YOUR LIFE INSIDE AND OUTSIDE OF THE OFFICE

INTRODUCTION

I never intended to be a successful freelancer.

I was an unhappy lawyer who wanted to escape a career I hated, so I quit to write full-time with a career plan that was murky at best. I thought I'd finally start (and hopefully finish) the novel I'd dreamed of for years, and write a few magazine articles here and there. While I had two published clips when I started freelancing in January 1997 (articles in *Cosmopolitan* and *Bride's*), I had zero connections in the publishing world, no journalism experience, and no idea of what to expect. But eventually I'd make some money, right? That was what I hoped, anyway.

It took me almost two years of full-time freelancing before I *knew* I could sustain a full-time freelance career. Along the way, I made pretty much every mistake you can make. I pitched markets I'd never read. I wrote horrendous queries. I interviewed the wrong kinds of sources for articles. I rewrote stories over and over—and over. I focused on what *I* wanted to write instead of what *clients* wanted me to write. I wrote vain, little essays that never got published.

Considering how many things I did wrong, it's amazing I survived those first couple years of freelancing.

But I did. And I learned.

I learned how to manage my time. I learned how to turn one assignment into a long-term relationship with an editor. I learned how to make the most of my time by specializing. I got over my fear of asking for more money and negotiated writer-friendly contracts that let me resell my articles to other markets. Over time, I branched out into lucrative specialties like ghostwriting, copywriting, and consulting. I published a couple of chick lit novels (although it took me a lot longer than I expected), wrote nonfiction books, and developed a speaking business along the way.

I started teaching writing classes, writing *about* writing, and presenting at writers conferences, and I wound up a freelancing "expert" helping others break into the business. Today I have more than fifteen years of full-time freelancing under my belt, and I make a respectable income even though I work part-time hours (I have two little kids who are my first priority).

I recently realized, however, that my success wasn't due to my persistence or even to luck. It's because as I gained experience I discovered the "secrets" of freelancing—the rules of success, if you will. Uncovering and embracing those rules took me from insecure, struggling freelancer to confident, productive business owner.

When *you* know the secrets of freelancing success, you can do the same.

PART ONE
MARKETING: SELLING YOURSELF AND YOUR WORK

When you think *successful freelancer*, what skill first comes to mind? If you said writing, you're wrong. It's selling—and that's why the first section of this book is devoted to marketing.

I've seen dozens of former editors dabble in freelancing only to return to staff jobs—and often the cause is their discomfort with marketing. If you can't sell your writing, you won't succeed as a freelancer. The secrets in this section will help you market more efficiently to both new and regular clients, and ensure a steady stream of freelance work.

1

BECOME A QUERY MASTER

If you want to freelance for publications (whether trade or consumer, print or online), you've got to be able to query, and query well. A query letter has multiple functions. It serves as a sales pitch, a letter of introduction, and a writing sample—and it's how you demonstrate that you understand the editor's market and can give her what she wants.

New writers often struggle with query letters, but the letters don't have to be complicated. I find that when you have a template to follow, you're able to draft compelling queries more quickly.

My template for a query includes a basic four-paragraph structure:

- The lead, which is designed to catch the editor's attention. It might be a startling statistic, a time peg, or an anecdote. Your lead should interest the editor enough to continue reading your query.
- The why-write-it section. This paragraph (or two, if you have a particularly detailed query) fleshes out the idea, demonstrating why the readers of the magazine will be interested in the topic.
- The nuts-and-bolts paragraph. Here you give the details of the story itself. What types of sources will you contact? How long will the story be? Will it have sidebars, and if so, how many? What section of the magazine will the story fit in? What's the working title?
- The I'm-so-great paragraph, or ISG. Here you highlight your relevant qualifications, including your writing experience and background with the subject matter. This is the paragraph in which you showcase your unique qualifications and convince the editor to give you the assignment.

Because I have the structure down, once I have my background research done I can pound out a query in a matter of minutes. Here's a sample:

> Dear Anna Lee:
>
> It's a common conundrum. You've actually stuck to a regular workout routine, but you're still not seeing results. While "lack of time" is the number one excuse for not exercising, what's even more frustrating is making the time to hit the gym—and seeing no change in your body. What is the deal?
>
> The culprit may be multifaceted. Driven by a desire to burn calories, women commonly overlook (or deny) the importance of refueling their muscles with glycogen by consuming carbs (and protein, too) within the "magic window" that closes forty-five minutes after intense exercise. Without adequate refueling, your regular routine may leave your muscles chronically depleted, which affects your energy level, motivation, and workout quality.
>
> Inappropriate meal timing is just one of the common nutrition mistakes that trip up motivated, smart women in the gym. "Dumb

> Nutrition Mistakes Smart Women Make" will examine some of the most common mistakes, how they impact (or prevent) desired results, and most important, how to overcome them. I plan to interview experts such as Tom Holland, MS/CSCS sports performance coach, and author of *The Truth About How to Get in Shape*, and Nancy Clark, RD, author of *Nancy Clark's Sports Nutrition Guidebook, Fourth Edition*, for this story. While I estimate 1,500 words for this story, that's flexible depending on your needs.
>
> Interested in this story for your "Health & Nutrition" section? I've written for *Oxygen* before and have been a full-time freelancer for more than a decade; my work has also appeared in magazines including *Redbook, Self, Health, Continental, Fitness, Woman's Day,* and *Shape*. Please let me know if you have any questions about this pitch, and I'll be in touch soon with another story idea as well.
>
> All best,
> Kelly James-Enger

That's it. Catch the editor's attention, make the case for your story, tell the editor how you plan to approach it, and demonstrate why you're qualified to write the piece. Include all four elements in every query and I guarantee you'll see better results.

FOCUS ON THE FRONT

New freelancers always want to know which markets are more open to using less-experienced writers. That's a tricky question. In general, smaller markets (think regional, local, and trade magazines and newspapers) are more likely to use new writers simply because they don't receive as many queries as their national counterparts. Less competition means a better chance of getting an assignment.

When it comes to national magazines, however, there is a place where new writers should pitch.

It's the front of the book. Front of book, or "FOB," refers to the departments that run in early pages of the magazine. (In magazine publishing, *book* means magazine. Confusing, I know.) FOB departments typically include several short pieces on the same page that run about 50 to 400 words and are often penned by freelancers.

There are six compelling reasons why FOB is such a promising place for new writers:

1. It takes a lot of stories to fill the pages, up to about twenty depending on the market. That's a lot of assignments, even if they're short ones.

2. The editor for each FOB section must fill the section each issue. Every issue. Issue after issue. And that means she's always prowling for new ideas—and new writers—to help her do that.

3. The editors in charge of FOB sections are usually lower on the masthead; meaning they're newer to the magazine and are less likely than more-seasoned freelancers to have a "stable" of freelancers. [See reason #2.]

4. If a new writer screws up a story (or fails to turn it in—believe it or not, it happens all the time!), the editor is stuck with a pretty small hole to fill. She's not going to have to scramble to fill two or three full pages the way she would if a freelancer dropped the ball on a feature. So an editor is more likely to take a chance with an unproven writer on an FOB than a longer piece.

5. Established freelancers often don't bother with FOB pieces. We're paid by the word, remember? So, while I pitched and wrote FOBs early in my career, I've given them up in favor of better-paying features—and many experienced freelancers follow a similar trajectory. That means you're competing against a smaller number of writers.

6. FOBs give you a chance to prove yourself to both the editor and the magazine. As a new freelancer, I couldn't always get feature assignments with the magazines I wanted to write for. But after I pitched and wrote two FOBs for *Self*, I nailed a feature assignment—and the editor came to me!

One more thing—FOBs aren't only for new writers. They're also a great way for more-experienced freelancers to get their foot in the door with hard-to-crack publications like *Outside, Smithsonian,* and *O*. If you're looking to break into one of your dream markets, consider moving to the front—at least at first.

3

USE THE TWO-PART TEST

In 1996, I sold my first magazine article—to *Cosmopolitan*.

At the time, I knew little about freelancing. While I majored in rhetoric, I'd never taken a journalism class. I'd never written for a magazine. I didn't even realize I was supposed to pitch with a query letter. Instead, I wrote the piece and sent it in. That's the wrong way to pitch an article to a national magazine. [See #4, Submit queries, not articles.]

The piece was well written, but the reason it sold is two-fold. First, the topic, on surviving your last two weeks on the job, was a topic I had personal experience with. As an unhappy young lawyer, I'd changed jobs four times in five years. I was all-too-familiar with the discomfort of the remaining days after you give your official two-week notice ... and had a unique perspective on the subject.

But second, and more important, the topic appealed to the vast majority of *Cosmo* readers. Think about it—how many of the women who read the magazine will quit a job and suffer through that two-week waiting period before they move on to their next position? Just about all of them.

That's the two-part test I recommend new writers use to break in to magazine freelancing, especially when they have few (or no) clips to their name. And it makes sense—we've all heard the adage "write what you know." That's why I suggest new writers start out by pitching ideas that they have some kind of personal experience with or connection to—ideas they are "uniquely qualified" to write—and demonstrate that experience in their ISG, or I'm-so-great paragraph.

But that's only the first part of the query test. The second is to ensure that readers will care about the subject—and make the case for that fact in the query letter.

So, for a pitch to *Runner's World* on head injuries, I used a first-person lead to demonstrate my experience with the subject. (Graceful nymph that I am, I managed to fall and concuss myself during a run.) But I also included the fact that seven million Americans seek treatment for sports-related injuries, one million of which are head- or neck-related. That means the query meets the two-part test.

Finally, use the two-part test even when pitching trade or custom magazines, which are produced by a company to build brand loyalty among customers. You want the editor to recognize that you "get" his readership and his needs. Here's a pitch that sold to a trade magazine for a personal training trade publication:

> Dear Christine:
>
> As an ACE-certified trainer, you work with a variety of clients. Some are new to working out and simply want to get into a healthy exercise groove; others are committed endurance athletes looking for an added edge or a way to round out their training program. But these athletes are also at a higher risk for injuries. Distance runners in particular are susceptible to developing conditions like plantar fasciitis, Morton's neuroma, and Achilles tendonitis that keep them off the roads.
>
> As a trainer, you can develop a plan to help these clients stay fit even when they can't perform their exercise of choice. But what about the emotional impact of being unable to run (or bike, or swim)? A study published last year revealed that regular exercisers who experienced forced exercise withdrawal also had increased negative mood and fatigue. Another earlier study found that regular exercisers experienced depressed mood and fatigue in as little as a week without their thrice-weekly workouts.
>
> "Buzz-Killed: Helping Clients Deal With Exercise Withdrawal" will explain the link between regular exercise and elevated mood and decreased anxiety, and more important, help regular exercisers manage the emotional changes that can occur during a forced layoff.
>
> Interested in this story as a feature in *ACE Certified News?* I estimate 1,000 words for this piece, but that's flexible depending on your needs. In addition to being an ACE-certified person-

al trainer, I've been a freelance journalist for twelve-plus years and have written for more than fifty national magazines including *Runner's World, Redbook, Health, Self, Fitness, Shape,* and *Chicago Athlete.* As a runner of twenty-plus years who has faced injuries and forced time off, I believe my recent experience will help bring a unique perspective to this piece (for example, I found that cross training helps me cope but doesn't produce the same buzz as a run), and I hope you'll find it's appropriate for a future issue of your magazine.

Christine, please let me know if you have any questions about this story idea or would like to see clips of my work; otherwise, I'll follow up on it in a few weeks. Many thanks for your time, and I hope we'll have the chance to work together soon.

All best,
Kelly James-Enger

Remember that a great idea is only the beginning. Your query should describe why you're uniquely qualified to write the piece and why the publication's readers will be interested in it. Meeting that two-part test will boost your chances of selling your story.

SUBMIT QUERIES, NOT ARTICLES

Hate writing queries? You're not alone—new freelancers often despair over queries and experienced writers get sick of having to send them. It can seem like a lot of time and work to pitch an idea that may ultimately be rejected, but a well-crafted query increases your odds of getting an assignment, whether you're pitching a print or online market. Consider the other advantages to writing a query:

- It focuses your idea as you come up with the appropriate angle for the story. In addition, as you flesh out your query you may come up with other approaches you hadn't considered. You can then reslant the idea to other markets, maximizing your time.

- It forces you to do background research—unless you're pitching a subject you're already well-versed in. What? You're not thrilled about the idea of having to do research *before* you even sell the idea? Well, consider that research makes for a more compelling query and is also likely to lead to other possible story ideas.

- It gets some of the writing out of the way. Often the lead to your query winds up as the lead to your story. As you work on the query, you're also envisioning the piece in your mind—including what structure it will take and who you plan to interview. When you get the assignment, you're not starting from scratch. A lot of the work is already in the bag.

- It improves your writing. Most freelancers start out with vague, poorly focused queries. (I sure did!) As you draft more queries, though, they improve along with the rest of your writing. If you've been freelancing for more than a year or two, take a look at some of your earlier queries. I guarantee you'll see a difference.

Besides, writing a query shows that you understand the publishing business. Professional freelancers query article topics—they don't write a piece, send it in, and pray. Submitting a completed article looks amateurish, and most national magazines don't accept unsolicited submissions. (The exception is if you're pitching an essay, in which case you send in the completed piece. That's because the editor needs to read the actual essay so she can determine if she wants to buy it.) Show the editor you're a serious freelancer, not just a reader of the publication, by querying her.

Remember, too, that your editor may have already assigned a piece on the subject or have a similar piece in her inventory. You don't want to spend time writing a piece that has no chance of selling because your editor is already covering it.

Finally, writing queries saves you precious marketing time. When you write an article, even a short one, you make dozens of decisions. You choose the topic, the angle, the length, the structure, the number and type of sources, and the tone—and you write the piece. What are the chances you're going to make all the same choices with your story that the editor would when you're basically writing in the dark? Slim to none.

A query tells your editor how you plan to approach the piece but lets her have the final say. Maybe she wants more words, or fewer. Maybe she likes the basic idea but wants you to take a different angle. Or maybe she wants you to use a real-person source, not just an expert. Don't try to guess what an editor wants. Give her a chance to assign you the story she wants instead.

KEEP AN LOI IN YOUR ARSENAL

As a freelancer, you often send queries to pitch an editor or potential client. But there's another weapon you should include in your freelance arsenal—a letter of introduction, or LOI. Rather than pitching a specific idea, you use an LOI to pitch yourself as a writer to a potential client.

In some instances, you'll know something about the market or client you're pitching, and you can customize your LOI to reflect that fact. But what about when you're pitching "blind," meaning you have no information about the market? Then you do the best with what you have, and highlight the qualifications that are likely to make you stand out from the pack.

Here's an LOI I sent to a post on craigslist seeking health/wellness writers. This pitch resulted in multiple assignments for a custom publisher. I've included comments about the LOI in brackets:

> Dear Sir or Madam:
>
> I'm replying to your craigslist.org ad seeking experienced writers who can cover health and wellness stories. I'm sure you're inundated with responses, so I'll keep this brief. I'm a full-time freelance journalist who specializes in health, fitness, nutrition, and wellness pieces; my work has appeared in more than fifty national magazines including *Self, Fitness, Muscle Media, American Health & Fitness, Shape,*

Woman's Day, Redbook, and *Family Circle*. I've attached two recent articles to give you a feel for my writing style. [Simple, yet effective. I've described my relevant background and attached the two writing samples the ad requested. This lets the editor know that I'm good at following directions!]

I'm a skilled researcher and writer, and know how to translate complicated health topics into "plain English" for a lay audience. I'm also an ACE-certified personal trainer, and speak and consult about subjects ranging from time management to goal setting to getting (and staying) fit. (That's the "BodyWise" part of my business.) I enjoy helping people make positive changes in their lives through my work as an author, journalist, and speaker. [The ad is looking for writers who can write about health and fitness and my background as a personal trainer gives me a unique perspective on the subject. If I were pitching a parenting magazine or business magazine, I'd probably omit this. Also note that I make no mention of my book-writing or ghostwriting experience. It's simply not relevant for this LOI, and I want to keep it short and sweet.]

What else should you know? I'm reliable, professional, and easy to work with, and strive to give my clients just what they want. It sounds like I have the background and experience you're looking for, but if you have any questions about my skills, please let me know. [I always have a paragraph like this in my LOIs. When I pitch a ghostwriting client, I mention my sense of humor and my pleasure in collaborating. Here I'm letting the editor know that I'm just the kind of reliable freelancer he's looking for.] Many thanks for your time, and I look forward to hearing from you soon.

All best,
Kelly James-Enger

If you do more than one type of work, you may want to have multiple LOI templates. For example, I have an LOI I use for possible ghostwriting gigs, another when I'm applying for speaking engagements, and another for general freelancing work. Each highlights a different area of my expertise and experience, and hopefully makes the client want to hire me. A well-crafted LOI can do the same for you and your work.

6

MATCH YOUR PITCH TO THE MARKET TYPE

Want to freelance? Then you're probably thinking of writing for consumer magazines—the "glossies" you see on newsstands like *Time, Sports Illustrated, Woman's Day, Men's Health,* and *Parents*. You may be surprised to learn that the most lucrative markets for freelancers are just as likely not to be national magazines, but their cousins, the regional and local magazines, trade magazines, custom publications, and online publications.

The kind of pitch you use for each type of magazine will vary. Here's the best way to approach each type:

NATIONAL CONSUMER MAGAZINES AND NEWSPAPERS

Most freelancers dream of writing for the big magazines, which pay $1–2/word. Newspaper rates aren't as high (and have been falling in recent years), but major newspapers pay decent rates, around $0.50/word. When you pitch the biggies, though, you're facing stiff competition. How do you get your foot in the door when you have few clips (or none)? By pitching the FOB section. [See #2, Focus on the front.]

Regardless of whether you're pitching an FOB, a department (a regularly occurring section), or a feature, make your query as compelling as you can. You're facing more competition here than with any other market, so make sure you have a strong ISG and that your query captures the magazine's voice. Suggest the section of the magazine your piece belongs in so the editor knows you're familiar with his publication, and plan on following up with another idea if your first one doesn't get assigned.

REGIONAL/LOCAL MAGAZINES AND NEWSPAPERS

Regional and local publications are a great place to break in for new writers, but they offer opportunities for established writers as well. While these magazines cover the same topics as their national counterparts, they almost always do so with a local angle.

It's true that a smaller pub like *Chicago Parent Magazine* or *San Diego Family* won't pay as well as *Parents* or *Kiwi;* rates range from about $0.10 to $0.50/word. However, I've found that stories tend to be assigned more quickly and involve fewer editing hassles than national magazines, which means you can make a decent hourly rate for your stories. [See #61, Forget per-word rates.]

Writing for regional magazines can help you develop a portfolio and specialty, and give you clips you can use to break into nationals if that's one of your goals. To break in, pitch a trend story, a profile of a local person (or a roundup, e.g., four local celebs or five up-and-coming chefs), or find a local perspective on a national trend for a regional parenting magazine (e.g., how area families are cutting back on expenses and saving money).

ONLINE PUBLICATIONS/BLOGS

According to the 2011 edition of the *Standard Periodical Directory*, there are more than 6,500 publications available in electronic format only. Nearly 28,000 print publications have electronic counterparts. That adds up to a lot of markets looking for material, not to mention websites and blogs that pay for content and posts. The pay ranges across the board, from about $0.05/word to $1/word, depending on the publication. Note that I'm not talking about sites like eHow and Demand Media Studios, which pay pennies—perhaps $15 to $20 for a 600-word article, but online markets that pay more writer-friendly rates. [See #17, Say no to content mills.]

You'll want to pitch an online market with a query; remember that the articles tend to be shorter than for print publications and often include an interactive element, like an online quiz for readers. Make your query tight and focused, and match the tone of your target publication with your e-mailed pitch.

If you want to pitch a blog, check its guidelines to see what type of approach its editor/owner prefers. Some people want you to submit the entire blog post; others like you to query a possible post topic the same way you would to an online magazine.

TRADE MAGAZINES

The stories for trade magazines are aimed at people who work in a particular trade or industry. Some of these magazines, especially the smaller ones, don't pay freelancers, but most do, with rates of about \$0.20 to \$0.50/word. Editors at trades aren't inundated with queries the way consumer magazines editors are, and they're often looking for people who have some knowledge of their industry—and who can write.

Trade magazines can also be a source of steady work. Early in my freelance career, a single query to *Chamber Executive*, the magazine for the American Chamber of Commerce Executives, led to a three-year relationship, until a new editor took over. A one-page letter of introduction to *IGA Monthly* led to several dozen assignments.

In addition, your editor will often provide you with the sources she wants you to interview, which slashes your research time. And I've found that edits tend to be minimal, which boosts your hourly rate.

To locate trades, check your local library for *Bacon's Magazine Directory, Gale Directory of Publications and Broadcast Media*, or *The Standard Periodical Directory*. Each lists tens of thousands of markets, many of which are trade magazines.

To break in, either pitch the editor with a query letter or use an LOI. [See #5, Keep an LOI in your arsenal.] When querying, use industry lingo to show you know the business, and pitch an idea that will benefit readers. Whether you use an LOI or a query, play up your knowledge of and experience with the relevant industry.

CUSTOM PUBLICATIONS

Freelancers often overlook custom magazines, but these publications pay well, with rates starting at \$0.50/word. A custom magazine is a consumer magazine with a twist; it's aimed at a particular audience—say, Jeep owners or people who buy Iams Dog Food for their pooches.

In the past, custom magazines resembled advertorial vehicles but today many are high-quality publications that mimic the look and tone of their consumer counterparts, and help create loyalty between readers and the relevant company. Print versions are more common but online versions are gaining popularity.

To break in, send an LOI that highlights your experience with the subjects the magazine covers, or pitch with a query. Ask your friends and family to collect custom magazines for you, and check out the Custom Content Council's website at www.customcontentcouncil.com for possible markets.

Different types of markets require different approaches. Matching your pitch to the market will ensure higher success rates, whether you query or send an LOI.

DON'T TAKE REJECTION PERSONALLY

When you freelance, rejections are part of the territory. In fact, I don't tell students what to do if they get rejected—I tell them what to do *when* they get rejected. [See #11, Employ the 24-Hour Rule.]

But new writers (and even experienced ones) often wonder why. Why didn't their pitch sell? Why did the editor say no, or worse, fail to respond?

Chances are good that your query was rejected for one of the following ten reasons:

1. **YOU MISREAD THE MARKET.** Your idea may have been excellent, but it wasn't right for that particular publication. Remember, your query should answer the question, "Why will readers care?" If your idea isn't of interest to the publication's readers, the editor will reject it.

2. **YOUR EDITOR ACTUALLY LOVED THE IDEA.** She loved it so much that she's already assigned something similar to another writer or has a piece like it in inventory waiting to be run. Sorry, you can't do anything about this reason, but at least it's not your query that failed.

3. **SHE NEVER GOT IT, OR SHE OVERLOOKED IT.** That's why the follow-up is so critical. [See #12, Follow up on every pitch.] How can an editor respond to something she never read?

4. **YOU PITCHED AN IDEA THAT WOULD BE ASSIGNED TO A STAFF WRITER.** Make sure you read the magazine's most current guidelines so you know what kind of work is assigned to freelancers. Pitching something that would be written in-house shows that you didn't do your homework.

5. **YOU DIDN'T PROVIDE ENOUGH DETAIL ABOUT HOW YOU'D APPROACH THE STORY.** How long will the piece be? What kinds of sources will you interview? How will you structure the article? Will you include a sidebar or two? The more detail you provide, the easier it is for the editor to envision your piece—and say yes to you.

6. **YOUR QUERY IS SLOPPY.** Whether it has misspellings, grammatical mistakes, or other glaring errors, like spelling your editor's name wrong, your query isn't impressive. To an editor, sloppy query equals careless freelancer.

7. **YOU PITCHED TOO LATE.** In other words, you queried a holiday idea to a national magazine in October. Magazines have varying lead times, so make sure you've given yourself plenty of time (at least six months for national pubs) to pitch a seasonal topic.

8. **THE EDITOR HASN'T READ IT YET.** That's another reason to follow up on every query. You're not being a pest; you're being a pro.

9. **YOUR IDEA IS NOTHING SPECIAL.** Editors want *fresh*. They want *new*. They want ideas that haven't been done to death. To set your weight-loss pitch apart, don't query with a hook like "five easy ways to lose weight." A unique or counterintuitive spin, like "eat more, weigh less" or "laugh yourself skinny" is more likely to stand out—and sell.

10. **HE THINKS YOU STINK.** And he thinks your ideas stink. He thinks your work stinks, and he wants you to lose his contact info—permanently. I'm kidding. That may be the first thing you think of when you get a rejection, but this isn't why editors reject you. More likely you just had the wrong idea for the wrong editor at the wrong publication at the wrong time.

So don't take rejection personally, even if it hurts. Shake it off and move on to the next market for your pitch. When you find the right editor at the right publication at the right time, he'll say yes.

LISTEN TO YOUR GUT

I'm all about managing my time as efficiently as possible, at least most of the time. Regardless, though, marketing my business and "qualifying" clients—making sure that they have the budget and motivation to pursue a book project—takes a significant amount of time now that much of the work I do is ghostwriting and coauthoring books. Inking a deal with a ghostwriting client takes significantly more time than, say, selling a magazine article, so I don't want to waste it on someone who isn't a viable client.

But how do you know who is and who isn't a potential client? Often your gut will give you a hint.

Here's an example. One day I received an e-mail from a potential client's assistant. The assistant told me his boss, a very successful, very wealthy (his words) real estate developer, was looking for a writer to handle several projects. He'd gotten my name from another freelancer.

I called the assistant, who told me his boss insisted on meeting me in person. I debated. The trip would be an hour's drive, and I already knew I wasn't right for a couple of the projects. My gut said, "Don't bother." But my greedy brain said, "Very wealthy!" In other words, this guy has a lot of money to spend on an autobiography, why not spend it on me?

So I agreed, and a couple of days later put on my grown-up clothes and drove to his office in the northern suburbs. I met with the assistant and his boss, and it soon became apparent that I had wasted my time. Mr. Fabulously Wealthy began sketching out his plans for one of his writing projects. It would entail an incredible amount of time and work. I listened, took notes, and asked what budget he had in mind.

He wouldn't answer me directly. Then he explained (as if talking to a four-year-old) that the writer had the *opportunity* to make an incredible amount of money as the project grew in scope. I pressed, only to have him grow angry at my insistence that no professional writer (including me) is going to put her time into a project with the hope of someday collecting money. I told him that we expect to be paid for our work when we perform it. He waved me off, and I diplomatically suggested that I wouldn't be the right writer for this fantastic "opportunity."

Attention turned to his autobiography. Again, he fobbed off my questions about pay. "The great thing about this book is that the writer will be able to learn about my life, and learn how to sell," he said.

"And the writer will be paid for writing the book," I added. Dead silence from him.

That was my cue to politely depart the scene. I drove home, mentally calculating what I'd spent for this worthless meeting. Four hours' worth of babysitting. Gas for the drive. Expressway tolls. Lost work time. My usually positive outlook. I came home in a foul mood. I was mad at the man, but I was just as angry with myself. My gut had warned me during the phone conversation. But I overrode it.

Now I ask about budget before I agree to meet a client in person. And I try to remember to always listen to my gut. I suggest you do the same.

HARNESS SOCIAL MEDIA

When I started freelancing, there was no such thing as social media. Now it's all that anyone seems to be talking about. How many followers do you have on Twitter? How many connections do you have on LinkedIn? Are you using Google+ yet?

Writers shouldn't worry about social media, right? Wrong. No, you don't have to have ten thousand followers on Twitter (but if you do, I'm impressed), but you must have some kind of virtual network and know how to use it to help sustain your freelance business. As I'm a relative newbie to the social media phenomenon, I asked Kathy Sena for her advice about this ubiquitous tool. In addition to being a Twitter master,

Sena is a full-time freelance journalist for magazines and the Web (twitter.com/kathysena) and the social-media reporter for *Consumer Reports* (twitter.com/CReporter).

"At this point, if you're not on social media, I think you'll be perceived by many in the publishing world to be out of the loop," says Sena, who's also the founder of Bad Ballet, a blog and an organization for women who are "leaping onto their next stage."

"I have met editors, fellow writers, guest bloggers for Bad Ballet, article sources, and many new friends on social media. I use it to promote my blog and to find great new ideas to blog about. Book authors today simply must have social media as part of their platform (a public Facebook page, blog, Twitter account, etc.). Is it time-consuming? Yes! You do have to manage it and plan time for it in your schedule or it can take up your entire day. (Not good for your bottom line.) But it's necessary."

Sena confirms what you may already suspect—that without a social media presence you won't be taken seriously by a book publisher. But increasingly publishers of all stripes expect freelancers to understand social media and how to use it to your advantage. Some ask you to Tweet about new articles or post your latest work on Facebook for the purpose of capturing more readers. Because social media can drain your productivity, she says writers should use it deliberately—not as a procrastination tool, like many writers (including me) do.

"Don't pop in and out of Facebook every ten minutes, for example, or you won't get your work done. Use social media in planned chunks of time and then turn it off and focus on your writing deadlines," says Sena. "Have a plan for what you want to accomplish on social media so you are more focused when you are there. (And that plan may very well include just hanging out socially with your friends on Facebook a couple of times a day. That's okay!)"

While your approach may vary, Sena suggests that writers harness different social media for different goals:

- **LINKEDIN** is your virtual résumé, a way to present yourself professionally to editors, agents, publishers, and other potential clients. If you have worked with someone, don't be afraid to ask him for a recommendation on LinkedIn, and be generous in recommending others when it's appropriate.

- **FACEBOOK** public pages (formerly known as "fan pages") are great for promoting yourself as an author, for promoting your book, and for creating a place where fans of your work can communicate with you and with each other.
- **TWITTER** is great for searching for article and book sources via key words, for finding potential gigs (key words again), and for following editors, publishers, agents, bloggers, fellow journalists, and just plain interesting folks. Freelance writers also use Twitter to promote their books and book tours, their blog posts, and newly posted articles. And it's a great way to follow trending topics and develop article ideas.
- **GOOGLE+** is the latest entry into the social media melee. Sena is curious to see how Google+ will take off and how it will affect how freelance journalists use social media. The ability to put people in "circles" makes it much easier to post things for select groups. Sena can send something specifically to her eighteen-year-old nephew one minute and post something for her "writer" circle the next. She's finding G+ to be a great place to discuss things like tech questions and journalism issues, and to find people who want to share their thoughts in a way that she doesn't see happening on Facebook (as much) or on Twitter (at all).

Like Sena, I use LinkedIn as a virtual résumé and Facebook to keep in touch with friends and family and share photos of my darling children. However, I also have "friended" business colleagues, present and former clients, and editors. As a result, I don't post anything controversial, political, or religious in nature. I don't look at Facebook as a forum for my personal opinions but as a way to potentially build my business.

"Remember that you are being seen by many people on social media and you want to present yourself as a professional," says Sena. "Avoid the folks on Twitter who enjoy starting fights. Avoid getting caught up in Facebook games that will take time away from your workday."

Finally, be willing to try new things as social media evolves, says Sena. "I recently joined Google+ and it was a bit confusing at first, but now I'm getting a lot out of it and finding the people there to be very helpful and informative. And the G+ user interface is actually really smart and pretty intuitive. I'm glad I jumped in. It's always okay to try something new and to be willing to ask questions."

I suggest you look at social media not only as an entertaining time waster, but also as a way to promote yourself and your business. It shouldn't be your only marketing tool, but it could very well become one of your most effective ones.

SEARCH CRAIGSLIST FOR WORK

I've found work on craigslist.org.

Shocked? I can understand why. Every few weeks, I take a spin around craigslist posts looking for writers. The overwhelming majority of them are, quite frankly, ridiculous. I see rates like $.02/word or $15 for a 500-word article—but with the promise of as much work as you can want.

Really? As much poorly paid work as you want! Um … thanks, but no thanks.

But here's the thing. I have gotten work from craigslist postings over the last four years. I've written for a local magazine and a custom publisher that posted looking for freelancers. And I've found ghosting work from craigslist, including two book proposals. As a result, I've gotten good at deciphering craigslist ads.

Knowing what to look for will help you determine what types of jobs are promising, and which promise to do little more than waste your time.

Be on the lookout for ads that include (or ignore) the following:

- **A DETAILED DESCRIPTION OF THE EXPERIENCE REQUESTED.** Ads that read "new writers welcome," or "attention all freelance writers" are usually looking for any warm body that can string some words together. Same goes for "perfect for students" or "great exposure." An ad that specifies the kind of experience or background applicants should possess is usually a good sign.

- **MENTION OF COMPENSATION.** Ideally the ad mentions money, whether it's a per-hour, per-post, or per-word rate. Some ads may mention a specific project fee, and the amount of money compared to the size or scope of the project will help you determine whether you want to send an LOI. I've seen craigslist ads offer $400 for an entire book; I don't bother with those. Some ads will say "compensation commensurate with experience," or something similar. I usually give those a shot if the project is a good fit for my background/experience.
- **SKY-HIGH PROMISES.** These range from the opportunity to write a "guaranteed *NY Times* bestseller!!!!" to the chance to get in on the ground floor of the latest social media/money-saving/news/fill-in-the-blank site. When an ad makes promises that are too good to believe, well, they probably are. These ads almost always make loads of promises but conveniently omit any mention of pay.
- **A DESCRIPTION OF THE PROJECT.** An ad that reads something like, "looking for a writer to write a book; send e-mail with qualifications and rates" doesn't tell me enough about the project to make it worth my time to send an LOI. My experience has been that promising ads tell you something about the work the person is hiring a writer for.
- **REASONABLE EXPECTATIONS.** I've seen ads looking for writers to author a book in two months' time, or to write twenty articles in a week's time. Those are not realistic expectations, which tells me that the person posting the ad has no idea how writers work. I skip over those as well.

Read enough ads and you'll get good at determining which may be worth pursuing and which to ignore. Send an LOI describing your qualifications, and follow up in a couple of weeks if you don't receive a response. Taking the time to respond to an ad can turn into a lucrative assignment.

EMPLOY THE 24-HOUR RULE

When I started freelancing, I collected dozens of rejections, what I call "bongs." (When I was in law school, that's what my classmates and I called the polite form letter you'd get after you interviewed for a job and didn't get it.) All of those bongs may have been disheartening, but they didn't derail my career because I'd already decided how to address them, with what I call the 24-Hour Rule.

The 24-Hour Rule means that within twenty-four hours of receiving a bong from an editor, I would do two things. First, I'd resubmit the query to another market; I call this a "resub." If *Fitness* wasn't interested, I'd try *Shape* or *Self.* If *Modern Bride* turned it down, I'd query *Bridal Guide*. Nearly every idea I pitched had more than one potential market for it, so I tweaked the query for a different market (i.e., suggesting the relevant section of the magazine it would fit in) and sent it out.

Second, I'd send a new query to the editor who had rejected me, starting with language like, "Thank you very much for your response to my query about ways to stay motivated to work out. While I'm sorry you can't use the idea at this time, I have another for you to consider." Then I'd include my new query.

The 24-Hour Rule transformed each rejection into two new opportunities. Getting my original query idea out to another possible market increased my chances of selling it. A query won't do you any good sitting on your hard drive, after all.

But the second part of the rule—getting back in touch with an editor immediately—helped me build a relationship with him even before I'd gotten an assignment. Here's how I look at it: When you go to the Gap to buy a new pair of pants, and the first pair are pleated pants that look terrible, the salesgirl doesn't say, "Okay, bye!" She brings you more pants—flat-fronts, capris, hip-huggers. She will bring you pants until you buy some or leave the store.

So be the Gap salesgirl and keep bringing the editor more pants by continuing to query her. *That's* how I got assignments from markets like *Woman's Day, Fitness, Marie Claire, Self,* and *Family Circle* as a new freelancer. None of my first pitches sold, but I kept querying (contacting those editors within twenty-four hours) and eventually got multiple assignments from all of them.

Finally, the 24-Hour Rule also eliminated the question of "What should I do now?" after receiving a bong. Rejections didn't derail me; I simply applied my 24-Hour Rule and kept going.

If you're freelancing part-time or you're swamped with work, twenty-four hours may be too ambitious. Maybe a forty-eight-hour or seventy-two-hour rule will work better. But the idea is the same. You give yourself a specific amount of time to resub your original idea and pitch a new idea to the editor, and you stick to it. It'll keep your queries circulating and show potential clients that you're a pro.

FOLLOW UP ON EVERY PITCH

Several years ago, I chaired the mentoring program at the American Society of Journalists and Authors' (ASJA) annual writers conference. My job was to match ASJA members who were experienced, successful freelancers with newer writers seeking career and publishing advice. I did my share of mentoring as well, and I'll never forgot one "mentee" I met. He was an emergency room physician who wanted to freelance and had sent his first pitch to *Outside*. The editor didn't assign the piece (the magazine already had a similar piece in the works), but he had been impressed with the writing and asked him to pitch other ideas

The writer never did. Let me repeat—his first pitch as a freelancer was intriguing enough and well written enough to spark interest from an editor at *Outside*—and he never did anything about it. That's a mistake. A big one.

Failing to follow up is one of the biggest mistakes freelancers, especially new ones, make. You send a query to a potential market, and you hear nothing.

After a reasonable time (say, four to eight weeks), follow up. Send a brief e-mail that includes your original pitch, and ask if the editor is interested in the idea. If so, great; if not, let her know (politely) that if you don't hear from her in say, two weeks, you may market the idea elsewhere. That often triggers a response and shows that you're serious about your business and marketing yourself.

Here's a simple template to use, with my comments in brackets:

> Dear Stephanie:
>
> Hope you're doing well. I'm writing to follow up on a query (working title, "Sleep Yourself Thin") I sent you four weeks ago; I've dropped it below for your convenience. [Remind the editor which pitch you're following up on and include it in your follow-up (in the body of the e-mail, not as an attachment) to make it easy on her.]
>
> Would you let me know at your earliest opportunity if you're interested in this story for *Complete Woman*? If I don't hear from you within two weeks, I'll assume you're not interested in the idea at this time and I may market it elsewhere.
>
> [Here's another benefit of following up—you put the onus on the editor to get back to you. If she wants the piece, great! If not, I'm not going to sit around for months hoping for a response—I'm moving on, baby. I've found this tends to provoke a response, even if it's a "thanks, but no thanks." You can give a market more time to respond—say, three to four weeks—if you like. The idea is to give the editor (and yourself) a deadline.]
>
> Thank you very much for your time; I look forward to hearing from you soon. [Standard closing line.]
>
> Very truly yours,
> Kelly James-Enger

Make sure you follow up on every query. After all, if you don't bother to follow up on your own pitches, what kind of research job will you do if you get an assignment from the publication? Following up isn't being a pest; it's being professional. Follow up on every query and LOI in a reasonable time frame—you'll get more results and be taken more seriously as a freelancer.

13 CREATE A PLATFORM

What comes to mind when you think of *platform*? If you're a book author, or aspire to be, you probably already know that *platform* refers to your ability to sell a book. In other words, what your name and connections bring to a book project.

Platform is as essential to an author's success as writing ability and stellar ideas. "First an author needs a platform to convince the publisher that he or she can muster up advance interest in the topic that will result in eager buyers for the book when it is released," says Christina Katz, author of *Get Known Before the Book Deal: Use Your Personal Strengths to Grow an Author Platform*. "In today's tight book publishing market, if you don't have that, it's going to be very difficult to convince a publisher to invest in you and your book concept." Platform is just as important after your book is published, adds Katz; it helps you garner attention, interest, buzz, and sales.

However, platform isn't just for book authors any longer. Freelancers of all stripes are finding that a platform helps set them apart from other writers, making it easier to market themselves. "In the 'gig economy,' every independent contractor needs a shorthand way to communicate the value he or she offers," says Katz. "A freelancer's platform would emphasize value to the kind of client the writer is aiming to serve."

A platform is more than a specialty. Platform encompasses not just what you write about, but who your readers are—and how many of them know who you are and may do something (like buy your book, or read a blog post or article because you wrote it) as a result.

If you're a freelancer without a platform, you can start building one by thinking about what your clients (both current and future) need, and what you can offer them. Freelancer Meagan Francis, creator of the blog The Happiest Mom (www.thehappiestmom.com) and author of *The Happiest Mom: 10 Secrets to Enjoying Motherhood* (Weldon Owen, 2011), says platform is important because she covers a specific topic that she has personal knowledge of and strong opinions about. "I'm a mom—I write about motherhood," says Francis. "I know a lot of writers feel boxed in and limited by the idea of narrowing down to a specific focus. But for me—at least right now—it gives me much-needed structure and focus to my work."

Francis has been writing about parenthood for eight years. "I was always interested in mind/body, wellness, psychology, relationships, and self-help, from a mother's perspective, but could never figure out quite how to make that work for me when I was trying to make a living selling one magazine article at a time," says Francis. "At some point I realized that I actually wanted to be like the Martha Beck [a well-known life coach] for moms and that helped it gel for me. For now, it works ... in my case I am lucky enough that my platform actually encompasses almost all the other things I wanted to write about, anyway."

Once you've identified your unique value to clients, you can start building your platform by continuing to grow the one you already have or creating a new one. John Borchardt, a Houston freelancer who writes for magazines and corporate clients, developed a new platform to help him diversify his freelance work.

"Platforms are important to me in both writing for magazines and working as a technical writer for corporate clients. My original platform was writing magazine job-hunting articles customized to the needs of industrial scientists and engineers. I continue to write in this area. This builds on my work experience as an industrial scientist and engineer," says Borchardt. "I developed a second platform based on this same industrial background, writing articles on various aspects of science and engineering: energy, recycling, the environment, and global warming. More recently I have drawn on my industrial background as a technology manager to write articles on business management."

When you have chosen your platform, make sure you can describe what it is and what it means for clients. For example, my current platform is that I'm an experienced collaborator who helps health, fitness, and nutrition experts write books. That's a short, specific statement that describes my value to potential clients.

Second, make sure that you're spreading the word about what you do. Your social media presence on sites like Facebook, LinkedIn, and Twitter should remind people of your platform, as should your e-mail signature. The same goes for when you meet someone online or in person. Ideally, everything you do should support and continue to build your platform, whatever it is.

If you're resisting the idea of limiting yourself to a specific identity, remember that your platform isn't static. It can always grow and adapt as your writing career does. The key is that it reflects your unique identity as a writer and helps you reach clients who will want to hire you.

14 PITCH QUIZZES

While I've written and published just about everything (articles, books, essays, and novels, to name a few), I'm primarily a service journalist. Most of my writing is about how and why to do something. Think easy ways to get more veggies into your diet, how laughter can make you healthier, and how getting more active can also improve your sleep habits.

But even I get burned out on taking the same old, same old approach to topics. That's why I pitch and write a lot of quizzes for both print and online markets. Quizzes can be a fun changeup from the typical service article, and they're easier to write than you might think. In addition, editors love them—they're a popular way to test readers' knowledge of a subject and to share information in an accessible, often entertaining format. And they add the essential interactive element for online markets.

Obviously the style, length, and tone of the quiz should match the market you're writing for. My quiz for a woman's magazine that helped readers determine their "panty personality," or what their underwear revealed about them, took a very different approach than an article I did for a fertility magazine on the facts and myths about erectile dysfunction.

Once you've chosen the subject matter of your quiz (for example, "what's your money personality?"), consider the length and format of the quiz. Will it be a multiple choice, for example, or true/false? Also determine whether the quiz will be the main feature of the piece or an accompanying sidebar.

As with any other nonfiction article, you'll conduct background research; interview experts; and locate relevant studies, statistics, and facts before you begin writing. The more you know about the subject you're covering, the stronger the quiz will be. As you research the subject, keep a running list of possible questions and answers—this will make it easier when it's time to draft the quiz. If you're writing a self-assessment quiz, determine what "types" you'll be helping readers determine they are.

The first quiz I wrote was for *Fit*. It was a simple 1,000-word story called, "Determine Your Workout Personality." The concept was that each of us falls into one of four different workout types, and once you determine yours, you'll know what kind of exercise you'll enjoy. I created the four "types" from years of working out at gyms:

- **SOCIAL BUTTERFLY.** The gym is part of her social life, and she loves group classes and working out with a buddy.
- **CONTROL FREAK.** This is the person who arrives with her workout in mind. Get in her way or make her wait for a particular machine and she gets annoyed.
- **THRILL SEEKER.** Easily bored, this one needs new challenges to keep her motivated.

- **COUCH POTATO.** This is the person who really doesn't want to exercise but knows she should.

After I created my four workout archetypes, I considered the various situations they might face and how they would react, and then I wrote the quiz. Here's a tip I came up with early on: If you're writing a self-assessment quiz like this one, order the answers in such a way that they correspond with the categories you'll eventually break the results into. For example, all *A* answers correspond to "Social Butterfly," all *B* answers correspond to "Control Freak," and so on. Or, if you prefer, you can assign points to answers (four points for every *A*, three points for every *B*, etc.) and have readers tally their points after taking the quiz.

Finally, write the quiz key, which conveys information to the reader. If you're writing a self-assessment quiz, the key should offer specific advice and tips geared to the different categories you describe. If it's a quiz testing a reader's knowledge of a subject, make sure you explain why the correct answer is the right one.

Writing quizzes isn't rocket science, and magazine editors appreciate freelancers who can enliven evergreen subjects with these kinds of interactive elements. It's one more way to help set you and your work apart from the other freelancers out there.

MASTER COLD CALLS

As a freelancer, you give up the security of a regular paycheck for the freedom of working for anyone you want to. That's a huge plus in my mind, but it also means that you can no longer rely on a boss to give you work. You have to find it yourself, and that means being able to sell—and selling includes making cold calls.

I know—you hate cold calls. Most writers do. But your willingness to make them may make the difference between a full plate of work and struggling to pay your bills each month.

As you gain experience and work for more clients, you'll find something wonderful happens. Clients start coming to you. You may not have to spend as much time marketing, though you should always devote some time to lining up new projects and client. Until you're so busy with incoming work that you're turning assignments down (and I wish that for all of you!), you must cold-call. That's part of freelancing.

Here are eight ways to make the dreaded task easier.

- **DO IT EARLY.** If you're like me, you start Mondays full of energy and enthusiasm. By Wednesday or Thursday, though, I'm looking forward to time off. I believe in "eliminating the ugliest," or doing the thing you most don't want to do first thing every day. [See #20, Eliminate the ugliest.] Get your week's worth of cold calls done by Monday or Tuesday, and you can take the rest of the week off.

- **WARM THEM UP.** Kristen Lambert, a Chicago-based freelancer who does corporate and PR writing, doesn't make cold calls. Instead she looks for some kind of connection with her potential client through LinkedIn or other social media, and she mentions it when she contacts the person, thereby transforming it into a "warm" call.

- **SET A REASONABLE GOAL.** Fifty cold calls in a day would do me in, but I can make five, even ten without losing my enthusiasm. Aim for a number that you can reach without killing yourself.

- **DO THEM ALL AT ONCE.** You'll save time by making all of your calls one after the other instead of doing them here and there. The more calls you make, the less anxiety you'll have about them.

- **WRITE A SCRIPT.** If these calls make you quake, make some notes of what you'll say and practice ahead of time. Speak clearly and slowly, and stand up—you'll sound more confident.

- **CHANGE YOUR MIND-SET.** Are you afraid that you're being a pest when you cold-call? Stop thinking like that. You have something valuable to provide (writing services) that the person you're calling may need, and may need right now! So get on the phone! Adjusting your attitude can make you feel more confident, which comes across to the person you're speaking with.

- **START WITH E-MAIL.** You know what a query to a magazine you've never written for is? A cold call. So is a letter of introduction. The difference is that phoning someone is much more immediate and stressful. If you prefer, start with an e-mail to your target and follow up with an actual call. Even if the person hasn't read your e-mail, you have a legitimate reason to call—you're following up on your earlier e-mail. This method takes some of the anxiety out of cold calls for me.
- **REWARD YOURSELF.** If I have to choose between the carrot and the stick, I can tell you that the carrot is a lot more powerful (and fun) motivator. Give yourself a treat—a glass of wine, a late-afternoon movie, a massage—for making your quota of cold calls, and next time you may even look forward to doing them.

Cold calls may not be your favorite part of marketing, but if you don't have enough work, you have no excuse for not making them. Use sites like Google to research companies, nonprofits, and other potential clients. Check their websites for the name of the person who hires or would be in charge of hiring freelancers, such as the communications director or publications manager; if you can't find it or aren't sure who the person is, call the company and ask. When you have the person's name and number, pick up the phone. The worst the person can say is no or that the company is not hiring freelancers. On the other hand, that call may turn into your introduction to a new client.

WRITE FOR BUSINESSES

Many writers are drawn to freelancing because they want to write magazine articles and books, and that's great. But if you want to make more money as a freelancer, don't overlook one of the most lucrative writing niches there is: freelancing for businesses and corporations.

It used to be that a "real" journalist wouldn't consider doing public relations or corporate writing. It wasn't seemly. Now that's changing, and plenty of freelancers are finding that business writing can boost their income. More writers are branching out into various types of corporate work, whether it's writing for external or internal corporate publications, or doing public relations or marketing work.

You needn't have an MBA to write for businesses, but you do need to understand your clients' needs and be able to deliver what they want. If you've never written ad copy, for example, you'll need to get up to speed on the difference between features and benefits and know what a "call to action" is. Features are the elements of a product or service, and benefits are the impact those elements have on the customers' lives. For example, a 2011 Chevrolet Corvette Convertible may have a 6.2 Liter 430-hp V8 engine. That's a feature. A benefit of the same car to the fifty-something-year-old man who considers buying it might be the way it attracts young women or how it hearkens back to the days of his youth. The call to action is what spurs the reader or listener to do something, whether it's making a phone call or purchasing the product. (Check out *The Everything Guide to Writing Copy* by Steve Slaunwhite or Peter Bowerman's books on business writing, mentioned below, for more on copywriting.)

In the past, companies tended to use local writers for work, but today you're just as likely to work for a long-distance client if you can impress them with your portfolio and experience. Starting out, offer to write complimentary brochures, advertisements, or website copy for a small company you have a contact with (you can help out a family business!) or a nonprofit organization to create some samples for your portfolio. Companies will want to see samples of your work before they hire you, so this is one situation where I'd disregard my never-write-for-free rule. In fact, I did a lot of volunteer work for Big Brothers/Big Sisters as a new freelancer so I had samples to show potential business clients. You needn't reveal to a potential client that you did the work for no pay.

Unless you have an in with a potential client, plan to cold-call to get started in business writing. That's how Peter Bowerman, author of *The Well-Fed Writer: Financial Self-Sufficiency as a Freelance Writer in Six Months or Less* and *The Well-Fed Writer: Back for Seconds,* built his highly successful corporate freelancing career from scratch. "The law of averages absolutely, categorically works," he says. "If you make enough calls, you will get the business." [See #15, Master cold calls.]

After you've introduced yourself to a potential client, ask whether you can meet in person or send samples of your work. Be prepared to quote an hourly rate, as most corporate clients pay per hour or per project instead of per word. Experienced copywriters charge hourly rates of $100-150 and up, depending on their expertise. Starting out, I'd suggest $50 to $75/hour as a fair rate for new writers, assuming you have some experience.

What do corporate and business clients want? First, they want you to understand their business. That means you should know what they sell, who their competition is, and how they position themselves. Before you make a cold call, you should have done some research on the company so you're not stuck if the person you're calling asks what you can do for them. The more specific an answer you can give the better (e.g., when contacting a sporting goods manufacturer: "I noticed you have an online newsletter for customers, and I write articles about sports and fitness"). You want to make the most positive, memorable first impression you can make.

Still, though, the background is only the beginning. When working with a corporate, business, or nonprofit client, you'll need to question the person hiring you so you can deliver what he wants. You should know what type of product or service the client provides, and plan to ask questions like:

- How is your product or service different from that of your competitors?
- What features and benefits does your product or service offer? Which ones would you like to highlight?

- Who are your customers? Can you describe them for me?
- What is the purpose for the piece I'm writing? (For example, a newsletter's purpose might be to build brand loyalty; the purpose of an advertisement in local media might be to attract new customers.)
- Who is the audience for this particular piece? The audience may be the company's current customers, or it may be a different group of people.
- What kind of call to action would you like to make? The call to action is what spurs readers/viewers/listeners to do something, whether it's to pick up the phone to call and order or to visit a website.
- What message do you want the audience to remember?

Use these questions as a starting point and remember that the more you know about your client, the better you can serve him. I wrote a lot of brochures for small businesses when I started freelancing, and I made sure that I understood each business and what it did before I started a draft. I often had to remind clients that their potential and current clients cared more about what the company could do for them (e.g., provide gorgeous landscaping that would increase their homes' value, add beauty, and make their neighbors envious) than the company's bragging rights to how many years they've been in business.

While the formats may vary, writing for businesses isn't that different than writing for magazine or book publishers. Research and learn what you can about your subject. Keep your audience in mind. Find out what your client wants, and deliver it. Do that, and you can add copywriting and business writing to your writer's résumé—and boost your freelance income as a result.

SAY NO TO CONTENT MILLS

During the last few years, there's been an explosion of content mills like eHow and and Demand Media Studios. The content for the site comes from writers who work "for cheap," if you consider $15 or so for a 500- or 600-word article cheap. I sure do.

Freelancers deserve to be paid, and paid well, for their work. Sites like these, which pay a ridiculously low amount for articles, are not going to help you build a successful career as a freelancer. The writing quality on the sites ranges from middling to poor, and your work there isn't likely to be taken seriously by editors and clients. And think of your opportunity cost—the time you're wasting working for tiny checks could be spent pursuing higher-paying clients.

When I see an ad on craigslist with a general headline like "seeking writers," it's often for one of these content mills. These companies are not looking for professional freelancers. They're looking for would-be freelancers, writers who are desperate to get published and think it's worthwhile to do it for $15 a pop. I hope that's not you.

So, do *I* write for the Web? Sure, if the rates are fair. My survey in 2011 found that 14 percent of freelancers are writing for the Web, and 8 percent are blogging for pay.

Writing for the Web usually involves fewer words than print markets, and therefore, fewer dollars. But there are thousands of paying markets for Web writing, with new ones cropping up all the time. The most recent edition (2011) of *The Standard Periodical Directory*, the largest directory of United States and Canadian magazines, lists more than 63,000 magazines, journals, newsletters, and newspapers. More than a third—27,927 magazines—have electronic versions as well and 6,554 publications are available in electronic format only. That's a lot of potential markets that need freelancers.

The Web's explosive growth means that companies, nonprofits, and millions of websites have been created, and many of those websites need writers. No, some don't pay well. Some don't pay at all. But others do, and companies launching or updating their sites often hire Web-savvy writers to provide copy and experienced bloggers to produce compelling posts.

If you want to make money writing for the Web, forget the sites that pay pennies or offer you "exposure" for your articles. (Why would you want exposure? People *die* from exposure.) Instead, look for well-funded websites that pay a reasonable amount for your work. Most of the Web writing I've done has paid $1/word, which is comparable to print markets. Rates have fallen in the last couple of years, but I think it's fair to expect at least $0.25-50/word for your work.

In addition to blogging, writing for online markets, and writing copy for websites, technology is creating new and lucrative opportunities for freelancers. Long-time freelancer Sam Greengard, who specializes in business and technology, writes and records podcasts for a number of clients. Typically the writer develops a list of questions, which the client reviews, framing the key points of what will be discussed. The podcast, in the form of a Q&A session, is recorded by telephone with a professional producer, and then posted online. In addition to writing skills, writers who do podcasts must speak clearly, and sound relaxed and interested during the podcast itself.

Podcasts. Blogs. Tweets. None of this media existed a decade ago, and smart freelancers are figuring out how to master different forms to stay flexible in an ever-changing market. I'm all for writing for as many forms of media as you want, as long as you're paid fairly for it. I hope you say no to content mills so you can say yes to the higher-paying markets.

18

CLOSE BUSINESS

Marketing starts with sending queries and letters of introduction, and making cold calls. But it doesn't stop there. People in sales talk about the importance of "closing" business, and freelancers must understand that as well. You need to be able to close the sale and compel the editor or client to hire you.

That's why sending a query isn't enough. Queries get lost, misplaced, and wind up on the wrong editor's desk. Too many writers give up if they don't hear back. Take a proactive stance instead. If you haven't heard from an editor within a reasonable amount of time, send a follow-up letter or e-mail.

I like to use language like "I'm writing to follow up on a query about the health benefits of fiber I sent you several weeks ago; for your convenience, a copy is enclosed. Would you let me know if you're interested in the idea? If I don't hear from you within two weeks, I'll assume you're not interested in it at this time and may market it elsewhere." This kind of follow-up usually prompts a response, and if I don't get one, I resubmit the query to the next market on my list. [See #11, Employ the 24-Hour Rule.]

While I've found that editors at national magazines and major newspapers prefer you to follow up by e-mail (they hate phone calls!), I do follow up by phone when I contact a potential business client, ghostwriting client, or smaller magazine, such as the ones that buy reprint markets from me. That gives me a chance to touch base, ostensibly to see if the person has any questions about my background. Sometimes I still hear "no thanks," but following up often closes the deal.

What if an editor likes an idea, but says she needs more time to decide whether to assign it? I give her a deadline and then e-mail or call her if I haven't heard from her. Of course I want her to buy the idea, but if not, I don't want her to sit on the query for months only to decide it's not timely enough, which alas, does happen.

The same is true with a potential ghostwriting client. A client who's thinking about hiring me isn't an actual client, after all. I can't waste my time with people who may or may not hire me. I will push a potential client to sign a contract, and if he won't do it, I'll "cut bait" and move on.

The bottom line is that marketing starts with contacting potential clients, but you must close business for it to pay off. If you're not doing that now, start—it will net you more work, and ultimately more money, in the long run.

19 MARKET CONSTANTLY

When you launch a freelance business, you spend the majority of your time marketing. As you develop experience and work for clients, though, you can expect to spend less time overall selling yourself. Still, you should plan on devoting a significant chunk of time, at least 20 percent, to marketing your business.

The way you market will depend on the type of work you do, which means that the strategies that work for a freelancer who writes for magazines won't work for a copywriter. That's why I suggest you create your own marketing plan, selecting different techniques that will vary depending on the type of work you do. Here are ten effective techniques to use:

- **QUERY LETTER.** If you write for magazines, whether print or online, a powerful query is your first line of attack. Every query should open with a compelling lead, make the case for the story, show the editor how you plan to approach the topic, and describe why you're uniquely qualified to write it. [See #1, Become a query master.]
- **LOI.** Second only to query letters in the freelancer's arsenal is the LOI, or letter of introduction. [See #5, Keep an LOI in your arsenal.] You should have a template on hand that you can customize for potential clients, whether you're contacting a custom publisher, a business, or a potential ghostwriting client. A "tweakable" template allows you to strike fast if you see a freelancing post or hear about a possible gig. The client will usually hire one of the first qualified responders, so you want to be as close to the head of the line as you can.
- **YOUR WEBSITE.** You need one. Period. Your website should be designed to attract your primary target clients. If you're writing for businesses, play up that aspect. If you freelance for magazines, include clips on your site and a list of publications you've worked for. At the least, your website should include a description of the kind of work you do, a brief biography, and contact information. You may also want to include a list of prior projects or publications or client testimonials.
- **YOUR E-MAIL SIGNATURE.** One of the easiest yet overlooked ways to market yourself is to create an e-mail signature that describes the work you do. Change it occasionally to highlight different aspects of your business.
- **SATISFIED CLIENTS.** Clients who are happy with your work are one of the best tools for marketing yourself. Once you've proven you are worthy, ask your editor if she knows other editors who are looking for freelancers. If you feel that's too pushy, at least ask

her to pass your name along to colleagues who might hire you in the future.

- **ARTICLE AND BOOK SOURCES.** I've interviewed hundreds of sources over the years, most of whom are professionals in the health and fitness fields. I let them know that I ghostwrite and coauthor books, and have had work come through recommendations because of the professional way I treated a source. [See #57, Make sources love you.]
- **ONLINE JOB POSTS.** Believe it or not, I've found good-paying work through online job sites. Check out Craigslist (craigslist.org), Elance (www.elance.com), Online Writing Jobs (www.online-writing-jobs.com), and Guru (www.guru.com) for freelance job postings. Yes, most of the work is low-paying, but there are legitimate gigs to be found if you don't mind trawling through the dreck.
- **NETWORKING.** Hate the word? Put a different spin on it. Don't call it networking. Don't call it anything. Just make an effort to create relationships with other humans, help them when you can, and connect. The person you connect with may not be a potential client, but he may know someone who is. The more people who know what you do, the better.
- **ONE-ON-ONE MEETINGS.** Every year, ASJA holds its annual writers conference in New York. Members can attend "Personal Pitch" to meet editors and agents. If you do a lot of work for businesses, it's worth it to join your local chamber of commerce or attend other local networking events to introduce yourself to business owners.
- **SOCIAL MEDIA.** Unlike a website, a blog isn't essential, but it can help you market yourself and your business. Same goes for your Twitter, Facebook, and LinkedIn accounts. Each should contain a brief blurb about the kind of work you do, again targeting potential clients. [See #9, Harness social media.]

Bottom line is to avoid a common marketing mistake, and one I've made in the past. You get busy with work and you don't market for a while. Then, after you crawl out from under your deadlines, you discover that you have to scramble to line up assignments.

That's why you should set aside some time, even if it's just a few hours a week, to market. That may mean sending out a query or two, touching base with your regular clients, or checking online sites for possible gigs. Consistent marketing will make for more consistent work and consistent money.

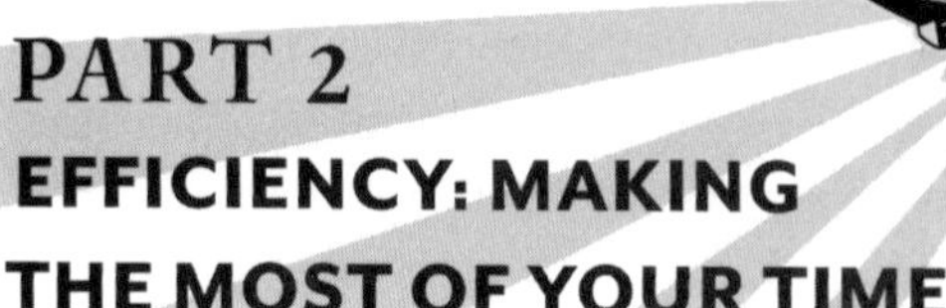

PART 2
EFFICIENCY: MAKING THE MOST OF YOUR TIME

You know how to sell your work? Great. Next comes being able to produce that work in a reasonable amount of time. The faster you can research and write, the more work you can perform. Yet most freelancers overlook simple shortcuts that let them work more efficiently and manage their time more effectively, and that hurts their ability to make money. The secrets in this section will help you make the most of every minute, whether you freelance full- or part-time.

20
ELIMINATE THE UGLIEST

In addition to writing, I do a lot of public speaking on topics ranging from healthy habits to stress management to time management and goal setting. Managing my time as efficiently as I can helps me make a full-time living while putting in part-time hours, so I'm always looking for time-saving measures.

In the world of time management, there are two basic schools of thought when it comes to what you should do first each day. One school says to prioritize your tasks and do the most important task first, then the second most important, and so on. The other school suggests starting with something relatively easy to do; by checking off the first thing on your to-do list, you build momentum for the rest of the day.

I say both are wrong. The first thing you should do is to eliminate the ugliest. In other words, do the thing that you most do not want to do. There are several compelling reasons why. First, when you start your morning with the worst thing you must do (whether it's writing the draft of a complicated article, revising a book chapter you've been putting off, or calling an editor to request some contract changes), your day can only get better, right?

Second, when you have something you don't want to do and you don't do it right away, you spend a good part of your workday coming up with compelling (and increasingly more creative) reasons why you cannot do that thing right now. You promise yourself you'll do it after you have some coffee. No, you'll do it before lunch. Wait, your blood sugar is flagging, so you'll do it after lunch. Then you put it off until three P.M.—and nothing gets done at three P.M. Eventually you run out of steam, and you run out of work time, and you promise yourself you'll do the dreaded task tomorrow.

Here's the thing: First off, the dreaded thing did not get done! That's bad enough. But second, consider how much time and mental energy you wasted throughout your day, coming up with excuses (oops, I mean reasons) why you couldn't do it right at that moment. That's not only a waste of time, it's a drain on your emotional energy and leeches your productivity.

That's why I end every workday by identifying the thing I most do not want to do the next morning, and start every workday tackling that task. Eliminate the ugliest, whatever your "ugly" thing may be, and watch your productivity climb.

TRACK YOUR TIME

I call myself a full-time freelancer, but I'll let you in on a secret. While I say I work full-time, that doesn't mean I work forty hours a week. Early in my career, yes, I worked those kinds of hours, but since then, I've gradually cut back on my total work time. I have more regular clients, which means I spend less time marketing, and I've become much more efficient when I'm working. Since I became a parent six years ago, I've managed to run a "full-time" writing business putting in fifteen to twenty hours a week.

As a freelancer, your most valuable asset—besides your reputation—is the hours you have to dedicate to your writing business. Spend your time wisely, and you'll make more money. The idea is to strive for a lucrative dollars-per-hour figure (instead of dollars-per-word) throughout your workday, regardless of how many hours you put in.

Here's the thing: You can't determine what your hourly rates are unless you have an idea of where your time is going. When I was a lawyer, I had to track how I spent my day because that's how my firm billed clients—by the hour. That habit spilled over into my freelancing business. While I don't keep track of how I spend every minute, I usually have a good idea of how I'm spending my time—and how long different assignments take me to complete. That means I always have a good idea of what my hourly rate is.

If you're doing copywriting or editing, you may already be charging by the hour. But if you're paid by the word (like with magazines, newspapers and online markets) or by the project (such as for a book proposal or book), how do you translate that into an hourly figure? By tracking how you spend your time.

Some freelancers use software like TraxTime, but you can just as easily make a note of every task you do while you're working on an assignment and how long you spent on it, and keep the list in your story file. You may be amazed that you're not working as efficiently as you thought—or that you're actually making more per hour than you realized. Here's an example:

Assignment: Interventional Radiology article (700 words, $700, due August 31)

Date	**Task**	**Time (in hours)**
August 4	Background research	1.5
August 6	Locate sources/line up interviews	0.50
August 7	Interview Dr. Keith/transcribe notes	1.0
August 12	Interview Dr. Mendoza/transcribe	0.75
August 15	Start draft	2.0
August 18	Draft/finish and turn in	1.25

In this example, I spent a total of seven hours on the story, which was assigned by a custom publisher. In this case, the assignment came to me, meaning I didn't have any up-front research and query-writing time—otherwise, I would have made a note of that time as well. At this point, I've put in seven hours on a $700 story, or $100/hour, not a bad rate for a straightforward service article. (This was a subject I'd never covered before, so I had to do some background research to get up to speed on the topic.)

However, and this is an important point, if I have to make revisions or conduct additional research, that additional time will lower my hourly rate. So if my editor asked me to rework this piece, which took another ninety minutes, my hourly rate would drop from $100/hour to $82.35. That's still not a bad hourly rate, but I want you to see that the more editing I do, the less I make overall for the story.

Get the idea? Keeping a simple time sheet for each assignment will help you determine what you're making per hour. Even more important, it will reveal what types of assignments produce higher (and lower) hourly rates, information that can help you decide what direction to take your freelance career.

RESLANT EVERY IDEA

One of the easiest ways to make the most out of your time is to break yourself of the one idea equals one pitch concept.

I try to never write about the same topic just once—I "reslant," or come up a new angle on my original idea, as often as I can. Take the evergreen topic of changing the way you eat to lose weight. I've covered it with the following angles:

- How eating breakfast can help you lose weight.
- How eating more fiber can help you lose weight
- How eating more low "GI" (glycemic index) foods can help you lose weight.
- How eating more fruits and vegetables can help you lose weight.
- How eating more protein can help you lose weight.
- How using smaller plates and bowls can help you lose weight.

That's six ways of reslanting the same basic idea, and I remembered and wrote them down in less than a minute. Yet I wrote those stories at different times. An even more efficient way to reslant, and one of my favorite ways to "double dip," is to pitch two very similar ideas to different markets at the same time. As long as they're not competing markets [See #50, Choose relationships over assignments.], you're fine even if they both get assigned.

Here's an example. Last year, I decided I wanted to write about social media. Number one, I knew next to nothing about it and needed to figure out what the heck it was. Why not get paid to do so? Number two, one of my good friends had just written a book that discussed social media and I knew I could use her for a source (and plug her book as well). And number three, just about everyone I know spends part of their day on Facebook and Twitter, so I figured it was a timely topic.

I pitched the idea to two of my regular markets—*Chicago Parent Magazine* and *The Complete Woman Magazine*. Because I write for both of them frequently, a short pitch was all I needed. Here's the relevant section of each of the queries I sent:

> Dear Tamara,
>
> Okay, you asked for some ideas for May and beyond...I'm focusing on the CP reader as a woman *and* as a mom, not just as a parent, as I have in the past. Here are some topics that may interest you:
>
> 1. [Pitch omitted]
>
> 2. Your Online Identity: What Social Media (and How You Use It) Says About You. Millions of us log onto Facebook, Myspace, and LinkedIn every day, but is the use of social media helping or hurting your social life? I'll interview a couple of experts about this subject (including Sharon Cindrich) and talk about how social media can help support your IRL (In Real Life) friendships as well as how to know when you're going overboard with it. I'd also like to take a fun look at what certain things say about you (e.g., your choice of profile photo, types of posts, etc.). I think this would be a fun yet informative piece, with a sidebar on the most popular social media sites. Again, I'm thinking 1,200 words for the story.

3. [Pitches 3 and 4 and rest of query omitted]

And here's the pitch I sent to *Complete Woman:*

Hi, Stephanie!

Great to hear from you ... here are a couple of ideas for you and Bonnie to consider: Your Online Identity: What Social Media Says About You. Hooked on Myspace? Spend half your day on Facebook? This piece will describe how women use Facebook, Myspace, and other forms of social media, and what their use of social media says about them. (For example, your choice of profile picture, type of posts you make, what types of people you connect with online, and how often you check in with social media all give clues to your personality—and that of your friends as well.)

I'll interview at least one expert on this timely subject and interview several "real women" for the piece, which will be a fun look at this ubiquitous technology. I estimate 1,000 words for this light yet informative piece, but that's flexible depending on your needs. (I'll also give readers an idea of how to interpret potential romantic candidates' FB and Myspace pages as well...and what to look for in a promising guy as well as "red flags.")

[Pitch 2 and rest of query omitted]

See how I took one idea but created two different spins on it? While both pitches spring from the same basic concept—how to harness social media—they take different angles and have different audiences in mind. Get in the habit of reslanting every idea and you'll market more efficiently—and hopefully effectively as well.

WRITE TWO STORIES AT ONCE

If you're thinking about reslanting, you're probably wondering—what happens if you have two or more stories on the same subject assigned at the same time?

Take the example above, where I pitched a similar idea to *Chicago Parent* and *Complete Woman*. These are noncompeting markets, so the audiences for my articles—the readers of those magazines—are quite different. *Chicago Parent*, not surprisingly, is aimed at Chicago-area moms and dads. *Complete Woman*'s readers are women in their twenties to midforties who are looking for articles about love, sex, health, beauty, diet, fitness, career, and finances.

So I wrote two completely different articles about social media. One described what parents need to know about social media, focusing on how Chicago-area parents are using it to socialize, keep up on children's health issues, and create a new online neighborhood of sorts. It included a sidebar about whether you should "Friend" your teen on Facebook.

The piece for *Complete Woman* focused on the do's and don'ts of using social media as a dating tool, exploring issues like what a man's online profile may reveal about him. My sidebar focused on a woman who had connected with a former classmate through social media—and married him! (Readers love happy endings.)

The very heart of the idea—harnessing social media—was the same. But the angles, the sources, the approaches, and the overall articles were very different. Yet because I knew the difference between Facebook and MySpace and could define a Tweet by researching the first article, the second took little time to write.

To double dip this way without writing the same story twice, follow these five recommendations:

1. Consider the markets you're writing for (and their audiences) and create a slant specifically for each.
2. Use different expert sources whenever possible. (If you must reuse a source, get fresh quotes that are relevant to the specific story angle.)
3. Use a different structure for each story
4. Find new "real people" to include as anecdotes.
5. Write different sidebars that complement each story.

That's it! Keep these five steps in mind, and you can write about the same subject at the same time, without writing the same thing twice or upsetting an editor.

MAKE THE MOST OF YOUR WORKDAY

As writers, we're all given the same twenty-four hours every day. How you spend that time, however, will determine how productive you are—and how much income you can generate. Learn to maximize the way you spend your time, and you'll see a difference in both the amount of work you produce and what you collect from it. Here are five simple ways to get more out of your workday:

MAKE LISTS

Okay, I know you creative right-brain types are chafing at this request, but writing down what you need to do will make you more efficient. After you have your list, prioritize your top three tasks for the day (or week, if appropriate). I usually do this in the morning, when I'm drinking Diet Mountain Dew at my desk and clearing the mental cobwebs from my head. I figure out what the three biggest priorities for the day are, write them on my calendar and number them, in order.

In addition to this "must-do" list, you should maintain a record of your ongoing projects. Some of these may not have firm deadlines, but you don't want to forget about them because you're distracted by what must be done today.

PROTECT YOUR WORK TIME

Are you a morning person or a night owl? I've found that I write more quickly in the morning—in fact, the first few hours in the day are my most productive. By early afternoon, though, it's harder for me to focus and concentrate. I try to devote my morning hours to hard-core writing and save phone interviews, transcribing notes, researching and other tasks for after lunch. If you know you write better at night, on the other hand, plan your most demanding writing jobs then.

DELETE DISTRACTIONS

Let me just say, no one *needs* to check their e-mail every five minutes. But sometimes I do. That's why, when I have a deadline, I close Outlook, my e-mail program, and open it at the end of the morning and midafternoon. Otherwise I waste time reading e-mails (even if I don't reply to them right then). I also keep my browser closed until I'm taking a legitimate work break.

LEAVE YOUR COMPUTER

Speaking of breaks, research shows that the average person can listen for only forty-five to fifty minutes before his attention begins to flag. I've noticed a similar drop-off in productivity for writing, which is why I take frequent breaks throughout the day. Aim for a break in an hour, no less, and you'll get more done even considering your "lost" time. Just five or ten minutes away from the computer will refresh you. I try to do something physical—a quick walk around the block, a few minutes of stretching, or even a quick vacuuming break—that boosts blood flow and eases out the kinks from sitting all day.

STAY FOCUSED

This is my biggest battle—I'm easily distracted. But if you let yourself get sidetracked, you'll eat up time without producing any work. Say you're researching a story, using Google to hunt for sources. You get engrossed in what you're reading (freelancers tend to be curious types), and look up to discover you've lost a half hour. I'll set my watch or use a timer and give myself a specific amount of time to research a topic so I don't wind up spending my morning scanning celebrity blogs, one of my guilty pleasures.

While there are loads of tools out there to help you manage your time, I assure you that the most valuable isn't a particular software program but your mind-set. You have to make it your goal to be more focused and accomplish more during your writing time. Once you do so, you'll become aware of your biggest time traps—and happily, discover that many of them are easily overcome with some practice.

RIDE YOUR WORK WAVES

With limited hours to freelance these days, my productivity level has to stay high.

I only work about fifteen hours a week, so I try to average about $100/hour. That means that a story that pays $450 should take me four and a half hours (or less), if I want to keep my hourly rate high. I've had days where I've averaged much more than that. I've written four articles in a day and banged out more than 3,600 words of a book chapter in the course of a few hours. When I'm on, I'm *on*.

And then there are the other days. The days in which I can't get any traction. I try to start an article but the words won't come. I'll switch gears and try to write something else, but I feel stuck. I can't get it together. I can feel my work time slipping away, and I have little or nothing to show for it.

As a new freelancer, I worried that those "dead" days would spell disaster for my long-term career. Today, though, with fifteen years of experience, I know that my productivity ebbs and flows like my mood, my appetite, and my energy level all do. Most days I get more done before noon than many writers do all day. But I'm not a superhero. Inevitably my productivity takes a nosedive after three or four days of "jamming." (While writing this book, I wrote nearly 7,000 words over three days. The next day, I managed to pen a few paragraphs. My creativity was shot.)

Early in my freelance career, I would have tried to push through. Now I ride the work wave. When I'm firing on all eight cylinders, look out. I make the most of that time and crank out as many words as I can.

I can always edit later. If I'm editing or rewriting, I'll work until I must take a break.

When a dead day arrives, I choose work that doesn't require the focused effort that actual writing does. I might make a list of future blog topics, catch up on social media stuff, or search for potential reprint markets. The idea is that I do something work related even if I'm not as productive as I'd like to be.

Don't fight your dead days; they're part of even the most productive freelancer's life. Instead, ride the wave of productivity when it strikes, and tread water when the water is still. Another wave will come eventually.

26

SELL STORIES MORE THAN ONCE

According to a survey of full-time freelancers I conducted in 2011, a mere 3 percent of writers make money selling reprints. I was surprised to discover that this figure is so low; I love selling reprint rights to articles and took in nearly $7,000 last year in reprint sales alone.

One of the reasons I make so much from reprint sales is because I don't treat them as an afterthought. I think about reprint possibilities when I pitch an idea to a magazine. Once it's assigned, I'm already lining up potential reprint markets in my mind. And as soon as reprint rights revert to me, I send that piece out to my other markets.

Let me give you an example. I have a handful of reprint markets that purchase stories on women's health, lifestyle, fitness, nutrition, and wellness topics. When I write an article on one of those topics (for a market with a writer-friendly contract), I make a note to offer the piece to my regulars as soon as it's available. So, after I wrote a story for a woman's magazine on how to reduce your risk of breast cancer, I turned around and sold it as a reprint to two different overseas women's magazines ($150 and $300); to a small custom magazine ($75); to a regional parenting magazine ($150); to another regional parenting magazine ($50); and to a regional woman's magazine ($80), within the next three months.

Get the idea? Don't treat reprints as an afterthought. Think about potential reprint markets *beforehand*—as you pitch, and as you write—and you'll make more money for your original pieces as well.

It's true that most reprint markets don't pay that well, but once you've identified potential reprint markets, the actual marketing takes little mental effort. I'll make it extra-easy for you with a simple, five-step process to sell your stories more than once:

STEP 1: NEGOTIATE BETTER CONTRACTS

When I started freelancing full-time fifteen years ago, contracts were more writer friendly. Now more publishers than ever want all rights to your work, which precludes you from reselling that story—forever. (You can always write about the topic again for a new market, but that's an entirely new piece, not a reprint of your original piece—what I call a reslant.)

Even contracts that don't claim all rights may contain exclusivity provisions that preclude you from selling reprint rights for three or six months, for example, or to a certain type of magazine. So you've got to read your contracts closely ... and negotiate better ones when you can.

For example, even when an all-rights contract is forced on me, I always try to add a provision that lets me retain nonexclusive reprint rights to my work. That means that while the publisher is purchasing all rights to the piece, I still get to resell it or reuse it myself. I've had even the most demanding publishers agree (albeit grudgingly) to that, which leaves me free to resell the piece.

STEP 2: LOCATE REPRINT MARKETS

This is the big time suck when it comes to selling reprints. Where do you find publications that will buy them? Start with a market guide like *Writer's Market*, but don't stop there. Publication directories like the *Standard Periodical Directory* list thousands of possible reprint markets, divided into subject categories. I've had the best luck selling to regional parenting, regional health, regional bridal, and regional women's magazines. (Notice a trend? Smaller-circulation magazines are more likely to buy reprints than their national counterparts.)

STEP 3: MAXIMIZE YOUR SALES

I don't try to sell one reprint at a time. It wouldn't be worth it, time wise. But because I specialize in health and wellness topics (though I do cover other subjects occasionally), I've created a master list of work that lists several hundred stories, organized by category. Then, when I contact an editor, I include the categories I think he would most likely be interested in. (If I'm not sure, I send the entire list.)

As a result, I often sell more than one story at a time, even to a new reprint client. Better still, the size and scope of my list means editors think of me when they're looking for a piece on a particular topic. (Last month, an editor from an overseas publication contacted me to see if I had a piece on organic food. I did, and it sold for $300. Not bad for about fifteen minutes' worth of work.)

I customize my initial contact letter to fit the magazine I'm pitching; if I'm contacting a regional parenting magazine, I play up my parenting-related pieces. If I'm contacting a health publication, I start with my health-related pieces. I set out my list of available stories, and ask if the editor is interested in *purchasing* reprint rights to any of my work (as opposed to running them strictly for "exposure").

Here's an example:

> Hi, Amy—
>
> I'm contacting you because I know you occasionally purchase reprints for *Motherhood*, and I have several hundred evergreen stories available for reprint you may be interested in. I've dropped my list below; please let me know if you'd like to see anything on it. And I'm always happy to "tweak" stories to better meet your readers' needs or to fit a particular issue or theme, so keep that in mind.
>
> About me: I've been a full-time freelancer for more than fourteen years, and my work has appeared in fifty-five national magazines including *Woman's Day, Health, Parents, Family Circle, Shape, Fitness,* and *Runner's World*. Please let me know if you have any questions about me or my work, and thank you very much for your time!
>
> Sincerely,
> Kelly James-Enger

Reprint Rights Currently Available/Work by Kelly James-Enger

Available as of March 22, 2011 (latest additions marked with **)

Parenting-Oriented

** "Common Nutrition Mistakes of Smart Moms" (feed kids better) 850 words

"Keeping an Open Heart" (essay on open adoption benefits) 780 words [I include the rest of my story list here]

STEP 4: MAKE YOUR EDITOR HAPPY

Even though I'm offering a reprint, I still keep my editor's needs in mind. What do I want? To sell a story as many times as possible and make even more money. What does my editor want? A story that will benefit and appeal to her readers. That's why I often "tweak" my reprints to make them more attractive to editors.

For example, I had a weight-loss piece that had originally run in a women's magazine. By rewriting the lead (so it was about feeling beautiful as you slip into your dream gown the morning of your wedding instead of feeling confident in a swimsuit this summer) and making a few small changes throughout the piece, it became aimed at engaged women in their twenties and thirties, not moms who were struggling with leftover baby fat. Give your editor a piece that appears custom-made for her market and you're more likely to make a reprint sale.

STEP 5: KEEP IN TOUCH

It's much easier to sell to an editor or market that has bought from you before than to constantly search out new markets. Every three months or so, I update my master list, making a note of the newest additions, and send it off along with a brief e-mail to editors who have purchased from me in the past. The hour I spend doing so always results in a few more sales and keeps my name in front of clients.

If you write for specialized markets or on esoteric subjects, you may not have as much success with reprints. But don't ignore the opportunity they present for subjects with wider market appeal. Developing reprint markets that will buy stories from you on a regular basis is an easy way to boost your bottom line without the time and hassle of researching and writing new stories—making more money in less time.

BECOME A GHOST

Freelancers love seeing their names in print, so it's likely you've never considered giving up yours. I know that I never intended to become a ghostwriter. After all, why would I spend months of my life toiling away on *someone else's* book? No thanks. I only wanted to write my own books, and that's what I did.

I soon found, however, that the life of a book author wasn't quite what I'd envisioned. I was working long hours, yet making less money than I had before, when I wrote only articles. The reason was simple—the time I spent promoting my books left me less time to write articles and other books, which cut into my income.

Fortunately for me, a nutrition expert approached me about coauthoring her book. I found I enjoyed collaborating with her, but the real payoff came when we finished the manuscript. As the author, she now had to start promoting it—but I was all done!

That was enough for me. I decided to pursue coauthoring and ghostwriting, and "my" next book was ghostwritten for a client. (Typically a "coauthor" is identified on the cover while a "ghostwriter" is never named or identified.) Today, most of the books I write are published under my clients' names—and I'm making as much money working part-time hours as I did as a full-time freelancer.

You probably know that many celebrities and politicians use ghostwriters to pen their books. What you probably don't know is that most authors who hire ghostwriters aren't household names. Instead they're professionals (think physicians, attorneys, financial advisors) who want to add "book author" to their CVs to attract clients and establish themselves as subject matter experts—but they lack the time and/or ability to write a book. They're willing to pay, and often pay well, to get "their" books in print.

GHOSTLY ATTRIBUTES

The key to success as a ghostwriter, first and foremost, is an understanding of your role in the process. Whether you get cover credit or not, you're writing *someone else's* book. That means being able to collaborate and to set your own ideas about how to approach the book aside if your client disagrees with your approach. That's why successful ghostwriters keep their egos in check. You may be writing the words, but the book itself is your client's. And that means your client has the final say.

Besides a collaborative spirit, you'll need project management skills. Depending on the project, you may be responsible for conducting interviews and research and keeping your client on schedule in addition to writing the book itself. And when it comes to writing, you must be able to structure and organize material and capture your client's voice.

As a writer, you likely already know something about the publishing industry. That experience—whether you've already published your own books or have worked with editors before—is invaluable to you as a ghostwriter. The more you know about publishing, the more you can assist your clients, whether they're submitting their work or deciding whether to opt for POD (print-on-demand) publishing instead of pursuing a traditional publisher. You should also know why e-books are the fastest growing publishing option today and the pros and cons of true self-publishing.

GETTING THE WORD OUT

You have two basic ways of finding ghosting work—spread the word that you're a ghostwriter, and go after ghosting gigs you find. Make sure your website and blog, if you have one, says that you ghostwrite. Mention it in your e-mail signature. Consider subscribing to PublishersMarketplace.com ($20/month) for a promotional listing and a way of staying up-to-date on the latest publishing deals.

Check sites like craigslist.org, JournalismJobs.com, and FreelanceDaily.net for possible jobs. And consider your expertise when marketing yourself to potential clients. I specialize in health, fitness, and nutrition, and almost all of my ghosting work is for professionals in those areas. The idea is to start with what you know and let editors, story sources, and colleagues know you've added ghostwriting to your repertoire.

POTENTIAL CLIENTS

Besides celebs and subject matter experts, everyday people who want to get books in print but lack time or ability use ghostwriters. (These books may run the gamut from memoirs to novels to how-to tomes.) Book publishers, book packagers, agents, and corporations also all hire ghosts, though they look for experienced ones.

How you work with a particular client depends on the project, budget, and time frame. For example, you may interview your client and write the book from scratch, relying on your notes; your client may write some of the book while you write the rest; or your client may provide you with background material that you use as a starting point. It depends on how much work your client has already done (and is willing to do) and how he prefers to work with you.

That's why before you take on a project you should know exactly what you're responsible for. Some clients (like book publishers and agents) will have a set fee for a project; others will ask you to make a bid. Make sure you know what's expected of you, how you'll be working, and how long the book will be before you quote a fee.

When it comes to *how* you charge, there are three basic ways—by the hour; by the word or page (e.g., $10/page or $0.25/word); or by the project. Most ghostwriting clients prefer to pay a flat fee for the entire project, which is why you want to know what you're committing to before you say yes.

Before you start work, have your client sign a written contract. At a minimum, it should include a description of the work you'll be doing (the more specific, the better); how much and when you'll be paid (i.e., in certain amounts throughout the duration of the project); your deadline; and who will own the copyright to the book (almost always the client).

With signed contract in hand, you're ready to get to work. If your client hasn't created an outline already, that's the first step. Once he approves it, you start researching and writing the book itself.

Once all of the chapters are completed (or the sections of the book proposal are complete) and approved, I like to create one "master" document that includes everything—the final draft—and send it to my client for one last review. After he signs off on the completed manuscript and sends my last check, we're done—unless we're working with a traditional publisher. Then I stay onboard to handle any edits until the editor and client sign off on it.

When the book is published, my *client's* real work as an author begins. But as a ghostwriter, *my* work is complete—which frees me up to start on my next ghostwriting project.

Keep ghostwriting in mind, even if you aren't interested in book projects. Ghostwriters also pen articles, blog posts, and even Tweets, so consider ditching your byline in exchange for a check.

FIND FACTS FAST

I used to write for a magazine that was known for making some eye-catching claims in its articles. My editor assigned a piece with a planned cover line claiming, "Boost Your Metabolism by 200% or More With Our Fat-Blasting Diet!" When she assigned the piece, she explained that the piece would be based on a new study, that had found that eating hot peppers, which contain capsaicin, could boost your metabolism.

Sounded good—until I actually read the study. First, it was conducted over just a few weeks. Second, it included a small number of subjects who were force-fed huge amounts of hot peppers—far more than people would eat in the course of a month, let alone a meal. And third, the subjects of the study were *rats*. As far as I'm concerned this study didn't *prove* anything—except that it sucks to be a rat.

When you read lines like "Studies say...," "According to recent research...," or "Statistics suggest...," that research comes from somewhere. As a freelancer, you have to research article topics and report on that research. It helps to know how to find the info you need—and how to make sense of it—as quickly as possible.

If I'm covering a subject new to me, my first stop is often Wikipedia. Don't laugh! Last year I was assigned a piece on interventional radiology, or IR. A quick stop at Wikipedia described that IR is "a subspecialty of radiology in which minimally invasive procedures are performed using image guidance" like angiograms. Guess what? I actually knew what IR was—I just didn't know that's what it was called. A little more background reading and I was ready to start my in-depth reporting.

Often simply finding the right experts is all I need to locate the facts or statistics I'm looking for. One of my favorite sources is Help a Reporter Out (www.helpareporter.com), a.k.a. HARO. You send an e-mail request detailing what you're looking for, and HARO sends it to thousands of subscribers. This is a great way to locate people who are otherwise hard to buttonhole (say, someone who's been in three traffic accidents in the last year or a researcher working on an as-of-yet unpublished study).

ProfNet (profnet.prnewswire.com) offers a similar service for freelancers. You can search an extensive database of experts or submit a query specifying what you're looking for ("a master gardener with experience in English roses") that's sent to PR agencies, universities, hospitals, and experts.

Besides ProfNet and HARO, you can also locate sources by contacting relevant organizations and asking for leads. Google makes it easy, but you can also check out the three-volume *Encyclopedia of Associations*, which you will find as a reference at your local library. The encyclopedia contains 20,000 U.S.-based organizations that cover everything from medicine to gardening to hobbies to sports to charity groups.

After you've identified an appropriate group, contact the association, ask for the media affairs or public relations department, and explain what you're looking for. That person often can suggest a member who can provide you with the information you need—or may have it on hand. Use the same approach with universities; contact the public affairs or media relations department and request a referral to an appropriate faculty member to interview.

Don't overlook book authors who've written on the topic you're covering. Check Amazon for possible authors, Google their backgrounds, and make contact through their publisher's PR department. After you've identified your sources, contact them to arrange your interviews. [See #48, Conduct more compelling interviews.]

Background research is a necessary task for much of your work, just make sure you don't get bogged down with it. After all, you get paid for the words you actually write, not for the time you spend researching.

SWIM LIKE A SHARK

In addition to writing nonfiction, I'm a published novelist, and I've taught fiction writing before. One of the points I always emphasize to my students is the importance of writing like a shark.

One of my favorite movies of all time is *Annie Hall*. If you've seen it, you may already have an inkling of what I mean. There's a scene near the end of the movie where Woody Allen and Diane Keaton are on a plane, returning to Manhattan from Hollywood. Allen's character realizes the relationship is over and explains his discovery to Keaton's character like this: "A relationship, I think, is like a shark, you know? It has to constantly move forward or it dies. And I think what we got on our hands is a dead shark."

What does this mean for writers? Be a shark, and keep moving. Keep writing. Don't let yourself stop while you're writing a draft, whether it's fiction or nonfiction—you'll lose valuable time, momentum and motivation. Can't think of the right word? Need to add a statistic, quote, or example? Use the old editor's "TK" trick. If you get stuck, type the letters "TK" and keep going.

The TK means "to come"; it's basically shorthand for "fix this before it goes to print." Then, when you edit your initial draft, you can fix the

TKs. (The letters TK don't appear together in any word in English, which makes it easy to locate them by using the "find" function in Word.)

Novelist Robert B. Parker was credited with saying, "I can't edit a blank page." Get the words down. Write what Anne Lamott would call a "shitty first draft." Just get it down—you can fix it and clean it up and make it beautiful later.

I find that the first draft is always the hardest for me to write. That's why TK is so helpful. I don't waste time or get derailed searching for exactly the right word; I just TK it and keep going. So in a first draft, I might write something like, "According to recent statistics, TK percent of women who lose weight regain it in three months or less." Then, after the first draft is finished, I'll go back and find the source to back up my claim and incorporate that into the manuscript.

I introduce ghostwriting and editing clients to TK as well. When I have a question in a draft—say, I need more info from the client or want him to confirm that I have described something correctly—I put a TK there. For example:

> Students who don't eat breakfast experience more anxiety and perform more poorly on tests than students who eat breakfast. TK/Patricia, do you want to mention a specific study here?

The TK draws my client's attention to the relevant section and makes for faster collaborating.

Don't get stuck trying to make your first draft perfect. Just get *something* down and improve it later. Ease up on your perfectionist tendencies, if you have them, and just keep writing. Keep moving. Keep swimming like a shark, and you'll boost your overall productivity and your bottom line.

WORK WHEN YOU'RE NOT REALLY WORKING

I've been self-employed long enough to know that there's working ... and then there's *working*. The latter means that I'm chained to the computer. I don't check e-mail. I don't answer the phone. I don't log on to Facebook. I just pound out the words on the keyboard and get as much done as quickly as I can.

However, most of my work time is the former … when I'm working, yes, but not with that intensity. I'm getting some words down, but I break up the time with other things. I check my e-mail. I check the Amazon ranking of my books and see how many copies my novels have sold on Kindle. I throw in a load of laundry and stop downstairs to say hi to my kiddos. I take a lunch break. I work—but not that all that hard.

But there's a third category of "work," too, which I call WWYNRW, or Working When You're Not Really Working. WWYNRW is what I call it when I watch reruns of *America's Next Top Model* or *Chopped* with my laptop, well, on my lap. While WWYNRW isn't actual "work time," I use it to do things I might not have time for during my work hours, and that makes those work hours more productive. WWYNRW tasks tend to be time-consuming but take little mental effort, such as:

1. Scouting for reprint markets. I make between $5,000 and $10,000 a year selling reprints to regional publications, specialty magazines, foreign publications, and other markets. The majority of them I find through Google; I then send a brief LOI to the relevant editor. A five-minute investment may pay off with a new reprint market.

2. Touching base with my regulars. I'll scan through my e-mail, and send a "just checking in" note to editors I haven't worked with in a few months. I just did this last week and sold a reprint for $200, plus I got the promise of more work from several other clients.

3. Searching for new research material. I search on Medline for the latest journal articles on a specific topic—say, sleep and health. I did this several days ago and incorporated new research into a query, which I wrote the next morning. It's already been assigned.

4. Sending follow-up e-mails about queries I haven't yet received a response for, giving editors a week or two to reply … and making a note of where to resub (resubmit the query next). Then I'm ready to strike if the editor doesn't respond.

5. Keeping up with social media. I don't like to burn my limited work time to maintain my blog, Tweet, or keep up with Facebook, so I tend to do this at night while I'm watching TV. That way I'm still maintaining a presence on social media without using my work time to do so.

Your time as a freelancer is precious, and limited. Look for ways that you can work when you're not really working. Taking even five minutes here and there to WWYNRW can boost your productivity overall.

31 REDEFINE "FULL-TIME"

When I started freelancing, I put in a lot of time to get my business going. To get any business started, you must market, and as a freelancer, that started with researching publications. In other words, I read *a lot* (and I'm talking dozens) of different magazines, trying to familiarize myself with what they covered and find homes for potential story ideas.

I also spent inordinate amounts of time researching stories. Like many writers, I was worried about not having enough information about a particular topic, so I'd research and research and research before I started writing. You don't need a doctorate (or even a master's degree) to write an article, but it took me several years before I realized I didn't have to comprehend every nuance of a subject to write about it.

The bottom line is that I was working at least forty hours a week, often more, in my quest for freelance success. But it's not the amount of time you put into your career that determines whether you make money—it's how you spend that time. Once I cut back on unnecessary research, focused on a handful of markets instead of pitching dozens of magazines at once, and developed regular clients, I was much more efficient. Today I work part-time by choice, but I strive to make a full-time living—and many freelancers do the same.

Gretchen Roberts is a former newspaper editor who has been freelancing part-time since her oldest child was born. "Part-time just made sense for me then, and it still does. I now have three children ages eight, four, and one, and my schedule has changed with their births, milestones, schedules, and child care availability," says Roberts, author of the e-book *Full-Time Income in Part-Time Hours: 22 Secrets to Writing Success in Under 40 Hours a Week*. "I truly feel I have the best of both worlds—time to spend with my kids, but time to get away from the craziness that is raising three kids, and devote energy to my professional life. I don't consider myself anything less than a full-fledged professional just because I work part-time and am changing dirty diapers when I'm not tapping at my keyboard."

Still, with limited time, Roberts has had to learn to be extremely efficient. "I treat my working hours as prime time. I don't waste them checking e-mail, writing blog posts, posting my Facebook status. Well, okay ... sometimes I post my Facebook status," says Roberts. "But for the most part I try to really focus on paying projects, because if I lose sight of the big picture, it's too easy to fritter away a day, a week, a month ... and my income takes a big hit.

"Second, I plan ahead. If I know I'm going to have forty-five minutes while the baby naps, I plan a specific task or two for that time," she says. "If I have a story due, I block out three or four hours to write it. When you have less time, you absolutely have to be efficient about using it." That's why Roberts pursues bigger projects over shorter assignments that require her to constantly change focus, and works with the same clients over and over.

"Think about it: When you get a new assignment from a new editor or publication, there's a huge learning curve. You have to fill out a flurry of paperwork, learn the style of the publication, communicate in-depth with the editor or client about his or her goals for the assignment, and possibly do a revise or two if you don't quite hit the mark," says Roberts. "The second time, everything's easier. You're in the system, so no paperwork except for a contract. You've learned the 'voice' your client or editor expects from your work. The learning curve is lower, and you're a more efficient writer."

Roberts' attitude and efficiency has produced an income of between $40,000 and $70,000 working fifteen to twenty hours a week for the past five years. "I think writers have to know that this kind of income is possible, rather than settling for less because they figure part-time hours means part-time income," says Roberts.

I know writers who put in plenty of hours but don't make the money they want, and I know writers like Roberts who make full-time money in far less than forty hours a week. My point? Rethink what "full-time" freelancing means. It's not about how many hours you work, but how you spend them that determines whether you can support yourself with your freelance income.

WRITE ARTICLES AND BOOKS

I started out as a freelancer writing for magazines and newspapers, segueing into writing books a few years into my career. Later I added ghostwriting and coauthoring to my work mix as I found that I could make more per-hour writing books with experts as opposed to authoring my own. I've found that writing both articles and books makes me much more efficient and boosts my income.

Part of the reason is that I retain as many rights as possible to my work. That means I can sell reprints to articles, which results in thousands of dollars' worth of "free" money each year.

But retaining rights to articles also means I can repurpose them as I see fit. So, when I collaborated on a book with a client and wrote all of the fitness content, I had articles ranging from how to launch a walking program, to staying motivated, to exercise, to using a heart rate monitor—all of which I owned the rights to. As a result, I could use them for the book. Of course, I still have to rework my content to fit the book, but it's a lot easier than starting from scratch.

I've taken the same approach with the books I author under my own name, which makes me more efficient. When I sold *Six-Figure Freelancing* to Random House back in 2003, it garnered only a $15,000 advance. But I already had about 25 percent of the material for the book on my hard drive, from columns and articles I'd written for publications like *The Writer*. Repurposing that material meant writing the book took less time overall, boosting my hourly rate.

This double-dipping works in reverse, too. As I write a book, I often come up with ideas for articles. I may have to do some additional research and interview sources, but much of the background research is done, which saves me time. As a result, I can get paid for the book (through an advance) and for the articles it generates, which again boosts my overall hourly rate.

There's another reason to write articles, books, and even blog posts about the same or similar subject. Not only does it make you more efficient and boost your income, it also helps you develop a platform as a specialist in a particular area. (Yes, there's irony at play here—while authoring a book helps *create* a platform, you need to already *have* a platform to sell your book to a traditional publisher. It's a chicken-or-egg conundrum.)

Regardless, the most successful freelancers I know write both articles and books, creating a living out of checks of all sizes and projects that range from a few hundred words to 80,000-word manuscripts. Like me, they enjoy the challenge, satisfaction, and income that authoring both short- and long-form projects provide.

Starting out as a freelancer, you're likely to be writing articles and other short pieces rather than books. Just keep a book or two in the back of your mind. It may be a natural segue into another form that can produce income and increase your productivity as a freelancer.

OUTSOURCE WORK

As an attorney, one of the few benefits of my work was having a secretary. Regardless of the size of the law firm I worked for, I always had a woman who set up depositions, arranged court appearances, and answered the phone for me. No, she couldn't write legal memoranda (the supporting documents that accompany a motion) or appear in court or counsel a client, but she could and did handle all of the grunt work.

As a freelancer, you're not only your own boss—you are your own secretary and assistant as well. That means you handle the grunt work, whether it's conducting background research, proofreading, or lining up interviews.

Why not outsource it to someone else? Over the years, I've boosted my productivity by hiring assistants to perform a variety of freelance-related tasks, including but not limited to background research, office organization, proofreading, and fact-checking. The more work I can farm out, the more time I have to write, which is what I get paid for.

I realized I needed some kind of help about five years into my career. I wanted, not a secretary, but an assistant who could handle research and some organizational projects for me. I contacted a journalism professor at a local college and told her what I was looking for; she passed on the info to her students, several of whom applied for the position. I paid my first assistant, Jill, $10/hour. After a brief intro into how I work, I set her loose. Her initial tasks included:

- Conducting background research for articles;
- Reviewing my hundreds of "story files" (the folders which hold the research, interview transcripts, and other background for each of my articles) and creating a master list of articles, including word count, so I could contact potential reprint markets to resell my work;
- Sending an LOI to potential reprints for me to determine editors' interest; and
- Arranging interviews with story sources.

As Jill gained experience, I let her conduct some straightforward telephone interviews and write a few sidebars (after receiving permission from one of my regular editors) for several articles. She was interested in freelancing, so I helped her with query letters and she broke into several magazines while working for me. Eventually she graduated and got a job in publishing, and we've remained friends. She continues to freelance on the side.

Since Jill, I've hired another journalism student (who is now a graduate student in Portland) to do background research for me. Alyssa is smart and reliable, and cuts my research time substantially; I pay her $12/hour.

I've also outsourced other work. I hired a retired reference librarian to fact-check my first book (for example, double-checking websites and contact information) and paid her $25/hour. Today I rely on Valerie, a friend of mine, to proofread book proposals and books before I turn them in. She's a stay-at-home mom who's also a voracious reader and a bit of a grammar snob.

Not only does Valerie catch misspellings and grammatical errors, she points out discrepancies and awkward phrasing, which is well worth the $10/hour I pay her. Her skills don't end there, either—she also designed the covers for my formerly out-of-print chick lit novels, which I currently publish as e-books.

A lot of what I do—the work that requires my brain, my insights, and my creativity—can't be performed by anyone but me. But plenty of other tasks can, and I make more money by farming them out.

Consider whether it's time to pay someone else to do some of your necessary but time-consuming tasks. The increased productivity may be well worth the amount you pay an assistant.

34

NARROW YOUR FOCUS

Like many freelancers, I started out as a "writer-of-all-trades," covering every subject I could think of. When I went full-time in January 1997, I was desperate for clips and experience. So I tried to come up with as many ideas as possible, pitching dozens of markets in the process.

About eighteen months into my full-time freelance career, though, I decided to change my approach. I no longer tried to write about any topic I came across that I thought I could pitch. Instead, I started to focus on a handful of topics that interested me personally, and that there were hundreds of high-paying markets for—namely, health, fitness, and nutrtion—and began specializing in those areas.

In the years since then, I've met hundreds of other freelance writers and have discovered that the majority of the ones who make a good living freelancing full-time (say, more than $50,000 a year) have taken a similar approach. They specialize. Maybe they write about fitness and health. Or business and technology. Or food and nutrition. Or parenting and health. But regardless of *what* they specialize in, they've created niches for themselves. In a career that spans more than fifteen years, I've found multiple benefits to specializing. As a specialist, you can:

- **NAIL MORE ASSIGNMENTS**—even if you're an inexperienced writer. Specializing means that you have more depth in a subject than other freelancers, so you're more likely to get an assignment than a writer new to the subject.
- **MAKE MORE MONEY.** Editors and other clients will pay more for experience—and if you ask for a higher per-word rate, you can justify it with the fact that you're already well-versed in the topic.
- **PITCH TIMELY STORY IDEAS MORE EFFICIENTLY.** When you're freelancing, you must come up with timely story ideas, and specializing makes it easier to do so. You're not trying to keep up on every subject out there, which is impossible anyway.
- **SAVE TIME RESEARCHING AND WRITING.** As a freelancer, your time is your most valuable asset. When you specialize, you cut down on your research time because you're not always getting up to speed on a particular subject. Sure, you're always learning new things, but the learning curve is not nearly as steep.
- **BUILD A PLATFORM.** Today, this is one of the biggest reasons to specialize. Specializing lets you build your brand, so to speak, and create a lucrative niche. You're competing against millions of other freelancers. Developing a specialty makes you more memorable and helps set you apart.
- **SELL MORE REPRINTS.** Many writers don't bother with reprints because typically the markets that purchase reprint rights don't pay that well. But when you specialize, you can create an inventory of work you can offer to reprint markets, producing multiple sales. For example, in 2010, I had one reprint market buy seven stories from me for different issues throughout the year

for a total of $520. Another reprint market bought five stories at $150 each. Reprints take little time to market, and that money quickly adds up!

- **BRANCH INTO OTHER TYPES OF WRITING** (like books, blogging, and corporate work). I started out writing for magazines and newspapers. However, as a health/fitness/nutrition specialist, I've also coauthored books; ghostwritten books and book proposals; freelanced for companies like The Pampered Chef; and broken into motivational speaking on topics like healthy habits and stress management. None of those things would have happened if I didn't have a strong niche as a health/fitness/nutrition writer.

However, let me make one point—specializing doesn't mean you *must* only cover topics related to your specialty. I occasionally stray outside my niche and enjoy covering topics that are completely new to me. But the majority of my work—whether it's articles, books, ghostwriting, speaking, or reprints—falls under my specialty, which makes me more efficient than a generalist, and means I make more money in less time. That makes specializing well worth it for me—and probably will for you, as well.

One caveat: Consider the subjects you already are writing about, the markets for/demand for the subject matter, and the amount of competition in the area before you choose to specialize. Ideally you specialize in a topic that has a wide appeal and plenty of potential clients, like business, technology, or health, than something narrower (with fewer possible markets) like rare skin disorders or ways to cook with tarragon. The more people your specialty impacts, the more likely it is to be a lucrative one for you.

CREATE YOUR OWN TEMPLATES

Use your time wisely and you'll be more productive—and make more money. That's why I'm always looking for ways to save time whether I'm at the computer or away from it.

Besides doing things like "task chunking" (i.e., doing like things together—in other words, answering all my e-mail at once or running a bunch of errands in one trip), I look for shortcuts to make the most of my writing time. One of the most effective ways to make the most of yours is to develop your own templates for written pieces you use frequently.

A template isn't a form letter per se, but rather a model that you can tweak to fit your purposes. At the least, I suggest that writers have templates for the following:

- A query letter
- A follow-up letter
- A cover letter
- A letter of introduction, or LOI
- A simple contract
- An invoice

You'll find samples of all of these templates in the other secrets in this book, including one for a simple contract for an article assignment. But there's one more you should have on hand if you'll be doing any work for businesses or nonprofits, which often pay per hour, not per word.

In that instance, you'll need a simple hourly contract if they don't provide you with their own. Here's a simple template of one:

> CONSULTING AGREEMENT
> This agreement is made in CITY, COUNTY, Illinois, on __________ ________, 2012, between CLIENT and Kelly James-Enger ("KJE"), a self-employed writer and consultant. CLIENT has retained KJE to perform writing, editing, and other related services, and the parties have agreed to the following terms:

KJE shall provide writing, editing, and other related services to CLIENT and at a rate of $100.00 per hour. KJE shall bear her own ordinary business expenses including but not limited to telephone and fax charges, postage, copies, and mileage; upon agreement of the parties, KJE will be reimbursed for unusual or extraordinary expenses incurred by KJE in her work for CLIENT.

KJE will keep track of her time and bill CLIENT on a monthly basis; client shall pay each bill within thirty days of receipt.

KJE's relationship to CLIENT is that of an independent contractor, not an employee, and KJE shall be responsible for her own Social Security taxes and other federal and state income taxes.

KJE agrees to abide by the confidentiality agreement signed on January 21, 2010.

This agreement can be terminated by either party by giving thirty days written notice to the other party or by mutual agreement of the parties. If the agreement is terminated, KJE agrees to complete any unfinished work and submit a final invoice to CLIENT within thirty days and CLIENT agrees to pay any balance owed within fourteen business days of receiving said invoice.

The parties agree that any and all work KJE performs for CLIENT is a work-for-hire and copyright shall be owned by CLIENT; however, CLIENT agrees to allow KJE to use samples of CLIENT in her portfolio and for other marketing purposes. Any exceptions to this policy shall be in writing.

This agreement can be amended at any time by written agreement of the parties.

CLIENT	Kelly James-Enger
[Contact info]	[Contact info]

Feel free to use this template to create your own version—and make sure your client signs your agreement *before* you perform any work for him.

LOCATE SOURCES MORE QUICKLY

As a freelance writer of nonfiction, you'll spend a large amount of your time conducting research. After all, you have to learn about a topic to be able to write about it, and it's likely that much of your research time will consist of interviews with experts and "real people," or anecdotal sources.

You can cut the time you spend locating and interviewing sources without sacrificing interview quality. The first step is locating the appropriate sources for your piece. Decide what types of people you need to interview. I suggest that you always identify an extra source or two that you may not wind up interviewing in case one of your top picks is unavailable. If your background research has uncovered potential sources, great; otherwise, check sources like *The Encyclopedia of Associations,* colleges and universities, and online sources like HARO and ProfNet for possible leads. [See #28, Find facts and experts fast.]

Experts are easy. "Real people" sources, though, can be hard. So I'm pretty much shameless when it comes to asking friends, colleagues, and acquaintances for help. I'll start with an e-mail to my friends if I need a particular kind of source—say, a mother of at least two children who has lost weight by eating more fruits and vegetables, or a college student who just graduated with more than $100,000 in student loan debt and no job. If they can't hook me up, I'll use Facebook or Twitter to ask for help. The wider you cast your net, the more likely you are to find who you need, so don't be afraid to reach out for sources.

After you know whom you want to interview, make contact. I typically call and introduce myself, and then explain why I'm getting in touch. If I've been referred by an organization, PR person, or online resource, I mention that as well.

Tell the source what you're writing about, why you're contacting her, what you want to ask her about, and how much time you need. I don't conduct the interview during that first call, preferring to give the person time to prepare for our actual interview even if it occurs later that same day.

You can also send an e-mail to make initial contact like the following (my explanatory comments appear in brackets):

> Dear Ms. Smith:
>
> I'm a freelance writer working on a story on risk-taking for *Chicago Parent* magazine. [Introduce yourself/explain the nature of your story

and the market] I know you're a well-known researcher in this field, and think you'd make an excellent resource for the story. [Explain how/why you're contacting her] Are you available for a brief (10-15 minutes) telephone interview about the benefits of risk-taking for parents in the next couple of days? [Tell the expert what to expect and what your deadline is.] I'm happy to work around your schedule and look forward to hearing back from you soon.

Thanks very much,
Kelly James-Enger

Use these steps to spend less time locating experts and set the stage for more productive, effective interviews even before you conduct them. And give yourself plenty of time before your deadline to complete your interviews—you always want to have a bumper in the event that a crucial source has to reschedule.

37

MASTER SERVICE WRITING

I consider myself a service journalist. More than three-quarters of my work falls in the category of how-to, whether I'm writing articles, books, or blog posts, so I've gotten pretty good at telling people why to do something, when to do something, and *how* to do something, or how to do it better.

As a freelancer, even if you don't specialize in service writing, you communicate information through the written word. That means that at least some of what you write—possibly lots of what you write—will fall into the how-to category. Service writing looks straightforward but includes a minefield of potential pitfalls you must avoid. You'll write faster and more compelling service pieces if you avoid these six common mistakes:

MISTAKE #1: INSUFFICIENT BACKGROUND

You're up to speed on the subject you're covering, but your reader may not be. Don't assume too much. For example, I cover nutrition so I know what dietary fiber is, how it works in the body, and why it's important. But my reader may have no clue about it. Here's how I highlighted the difference between the soluble and insoluble fiber in a fitness magazine article:

> The two types react differently in water—soluble fiber dissolves, becoming gummy, while insoluble fiber holds water. "Soluble fiber acts more like a sponge," says Jackson. "It helps suck cholesterol out and lower bad cholesterol levels." Insoluble fiber acts more like a broom than a sponge, essentially sweeping out your intestines and keeping the area clean, adds Jackson. "They both play different roles but they're equally important in promoting general health," she says.

See how I've explained the difference between the two and given readers a mental picture of how they work in the body? Simple, yet essential for a reader who knows little about the topic.

MISTAKE #2: BORING QUOTES

Unless you're the sole source for a story, you'll rely on interviews for the piece. Regardless of whether you're quoting an expert or a "real person," make sure the quotes you use "pop." For example, an interview transcript with a registered dietitian for a story about how stress impacts your waistline included the following two lines: "Eating when you're not hungry makes people feel bad afterwards," and "No one feels empowered when they're on their third row of Oreos."

The quotes mean the same basic thing, but I used the latter—the language is more specific and more arresting. Choose direct quotes that are compelling and strong; otherwise, take the information out of direct quotes and attribute to the source.

MISTAKE #3: RETURNING TO THE WELL TOO OFTEN

If you write about a particular subject area, you probably already have your "favorite" expert sources who can be counted on to give you great information. But falling into a habit of always hitting up the same sources can hurt the quality of your work.

Make sure you include new experts and check what's happening on the topic, even if it's one you cover frequently. And if you write about ever-changing topics like technology or health, this is critical for accuracy.

MISTAKE #4: NO "REAL PEOPLE"

Yes, experts can explain *why* something is the way it is. But for color, and more memorable articles, include "real people" sources as well.

For example, in a piece I did on the benefits of eating breakfast, I reported on recent research about how eating breakfast improves memory and cognition—and boosts mood and energy. I included quotes from registered dietitians explaining why breakfast is so important. But I also included quotes from people who had discovered that eating breakfast gave them more energy and helped them lose weight. These "real people" anecdotes liven up a service piece and provide readers with real-life examples that they can relate to as well.

MISTAKE #5: INSUFFICIENT SERVICE

Just because *you* know how to do something doesn't mean your reader will understand it as well. Make sure you include the how-tos, step-by-step if necessary. For example, in a piece on toddler tooth traumas, I explained why parents should brush their children's teeth regularly. But how do you actually do this? I included specific tips like "hold your child's head steady," "choose a child's brush with extrasoft bristles," and "brush along the gum line, not just the teeth themselves" so that parents would be able to put the advice from the article into practice. With service writing, the more specific the advice, the better.

MISTAKE #6: SKIMPING ON SIDEBARS

Finally, sidebars are often a great addition to a service piece. For example, when I wrote a piece for *The Writer* on the effectiveness of letters of introduction, or LOIs, my sidebar included two examples of LOIs that readers could use as models. My above-mentioned piece on the health benefits of fiber included a sidebar listing foods with high fiber content, their serving size, and the total grams of fiber in each. I'd take a similar approach if I were writing a book chapter on fiber, too.

Service writing will never go out of style. Readers are always looking for advice about how to improve their lives, which makes this genre a lucrative one whether you write articles, books, or blog posts. Make your service pieces specific, interesting, and helpful, and you'll have editors and readers coming back for more.

CONSIDER ANOTHER CAREER

Wait, isn't this a book on successful freelancing? So why am I suggesting you consider another career?

Because it may make you more productive, and happier, too.

While some freelancers make all of their income from their writing work, and others work a day job and freelance on the side, there's a third option—pursuing two careers simultaneously. Writers who do this find that it helps prevent burnout and that the nonwriting career supports the freelance one.

My first grown-up career was that of a lawyer. About four years in, I started freelancing "on the side," and quit the law to freelance full-time in January 1997. Eventually I branched out from writing for magazines and newspapers to doing copywriting for corporations and businesses to writing books and teaching writing classes to ghostwriting and public speaking. To me, all of this falls under the "freelancing" umbrella.

However, about four years ago, I decided to add something new to my mix and became certified as a personal trainer through the American Council on Exercise. So far I train friends and family members, but once my daughter is a little older, I plan to do more personal training. I'm looking forward to the mix of writing and hands-on work.

Other freelancers launch two careers simultaneously. Psychotherapist Tina B. Tessina, Ph.D., was studying to be a therapist when she began writing her first book in 1975. She became licensed as a psychotherapist in 1978, and the book was published in 1980. Since then, she's been both a full-time therapist and a full-time best-selling author.

"Writing has turned out to be the perfect complement to doing psychotherapy," says Tessina, author of several books, including *Money, Sex and Kids*. "My plan is to keep my career as multifaceted as possible—as it will be more interesting and force me to stretch outside my comfort zone by building new skills and abilities."

Russell Wild had an MBA to his name when he started his first job, as a credit analyst at a bank. Deciding that banking wasn't for him, he quit to freelance. After a stint as an in-house editor and writer at Rodale, he returned to freelancing full-time. "By 2000, I was writing almost uniquely about finances, and in 2002, decided to go back to school for a graduate certificate in personal finance and to become a registered investment advisor," says Wild, a fee-only investment advisor, freelance journalist, and author/co-author of numerous books, including *One Year to an Organized Financial Life*. He's been juggling the two careers since.

A second career can actually feed and support your writing one. You have an entirely different work experience to draw from, and that work may lead to additional writing topics and assignments. Tessina's work as a psychotherapist gives her ideas and insights she writes about in her newsletter, blog, articles, and books. Wild says that his work as a financial writer gives him instant access to the greatest minds in finance, and that his investment clients give him "lots of grist for the writing mill," says Wild. "I know, much better than most writers, what kinds of money questions are on people's minds. I'm never hurting for anecdotes." In turn, his books on finance have ensured a steady stream of investment clients.

Of course, there are drawbacks to juggling multiple professions. The amount of time you may spend on each career may vary, and when both businesses are thriving, you've got the recipe for overwork and burnout. But if you still want to freelance and pursue another profession, consider how much time (and possibly, money) it will take to get your new business up and running. Do you have to go back to school? Get additional training? Get a business license or certification? In the long run, is it worth it?

Even with a background in fitness, it took me a good three months (and about $500 worth of classes, materials, and exam fees) to study for my certification exam—time away from my freelance business. I have to take continuing education classes to maintain my certification.

Yet the work I've done as a trainer has led to freelance assignments, and working in a new field gives me new insights and new ideas. Plus, I love helping people get healthier, and working one-on-one with clients. For me—and many freelancers—two careers are better than one. Consider whether another profession feels right to you, too.

USE E-MAIL THE RIGHT WAY

E-mail can be an efficient way to market, submit your work, and stay in touch with clients, sources, and fellow freelancers. It can also be a waste of your and your recipient's time unless you keep the following seven tips in mind.

SPECIFY YOUR SUBJECT

Your subject line should catch the recipient's attention and let him know why you're contacting him. When I'm sending a query to a new market, for example, I'll use a subject line like, "Query from Kelly James-Enger: Sleep Yourself Thin" If it's someone I've worked with before, I'm less formal: "Hi, Tamara/Several Timely Queries for You." I usually avoid using the word "pitch" in a subject line because although it's synonymous with query, it tends to make editors think of PR people, who also "pitch" ideas. And editors are notorious for ignoring PR pitches—just ask any PR professional.

If you have an in with the person, mention it in your subject line, like: "Jenny Fink suggested I get in touch/timely health reprints available," or "Enjoyed your panel at ASJA and have a proposal for you to consider."

KEEP IT NICE

E-mail has made communicating easier than ever before, but it's also made it easier to write and send something you'll regret. Be careful about what you communicate. For example, I recently received an e-mail from a fellow freelancer asking me about a publisher I'd worked with. I'd had a less-than-happy relationship with this particular publisher, and wrote her back and told her I'd be happy to talk with her by phone about my experience. Never put something negative in writing; you never know who may end up reading it.

AVOID ATTACHMENTS

Hopefully you know never to send an attachment unless it's been specifically requested. If you want to send clips with a query, include links in the body of your query, or ask if you may send them by snail mail. If your editor wants to see them, she can ask for JPEGs via e-mail. If I get an unexpected e-mail with attachments, I delete it if my spam filter hasn't grabbed it already.

WAIT TO HIT SEND

I know the difference between *too, two,* and *to.* So I was mortified to discover I'd sent an e-mail to one of my regular clients using one of them the wrong way. Typos make you look stupid, or at least sloppy, which is not the impression you want to make on a present or potential client, or anyone else for that matter. Proofread every e-mail before you hit send. And please do not write a knee-jerk reaction because you're angry, upset, disappointed, disgusted, you name it. Take the time to cool off before you send an e-mail you'll regret later. (See my above point, Keep It Nice.)

GIVE THEM TIME

E-mail used to be the fastest way to get in touch; now we have Tweets, IM'ing, and texting, which make e-mail seem glacial by comparison. So why do we expect a superspeedy response? It doesn't work that way. You may get a quick reply, but you probably won't. Don't send a follow-up note twenty-four hours later. If it's a matter that requires a fast turnaround, call. Otherwise, make a note if/when you need to follow up and move on to your next task.

MAKE IT EASY

Look for ways to eliminate unnecessary responses. If I send an e-mail confirming the details of an assignment, I just ask the client to respond with "agreed" if the terms are what we discussed. When I turn a story in, I'll write, "Please hit 'reply' so I know you got this okay." Yes, you can send a "return receipt" so you know the recipient received and/or read something, but those pop-up boxes annoy me, so I don't use them. I ask the editor to hit reply instead, which seems more polite.

PICK UP THE PHONE

Just because e-mail is available doesn't mean it's the right media for you to use. I wouldn't try to negotiate a contract via e-mail or ask an editor to put me on the masthead as contributing editor via e-mail. (I might send a follow-up e-mail in both instances, though, setting out my points or recapping our discussion.) And while some freelancers do a lot of e-mail interviews, my first preference is phone. Agreeing to an e-mail interview because your source requests it is fine. Requesting an e-mail interview (which means your source is responsible for typing up his answers to your questions) is not, in my opinion.

A phone conversation is often faster and less likely to be misinterpreted than an e-mail exchange. And in a world of e-mails and Tweets, "real" mail stands out. That's why I send thank-you notes and personal notes via snail mail. Yes, e-mail is quicker, but snail mail shows that you made an extra effort—and often that's part of what you want your recipient to remember.

40

PERFORM CPR

It's happened to just about every freelancer I know. You got the assignment. You researched the piece, wrote it to your editor's specifications, and turned it in on deadline. A week or two later, the editor requested a rewrite, or maybe two. But the end result was unexpected, and undesired. Your piece got killed.

What's next? How do you perform CPR on a dead story?

First, ask why. Having a story killed is unfair. At least, it feels that way. But be honest with yourself. Did you give the editor what she asked for? Did you follow the terms of the assignment, or was your story subpar? If you dropped the ball, admit it. Offer to rewrite the piece if you haven't already—better to collect the full fee for an assignment and have it run, than a kill fee. (Kill fee provisions vary but the idea is that they pay you a percentage of the assignment—often one-quarter to one-third of the original fee—and rights revert back to you.)

If you didn't, well, it's okay to be angry, especially when the piece was killed through no fault of your own. Stories are killed for unfair and nebulous reasons. Some editors routinely overassign and then kill the stories they decide they don't want. Sometimes your assigning editor leaves the magazine, orphaning your piece. His successor may decide to go in a new direction and kill stories assigned by his predecessor. (This has happened to me several times at three different magazines.) Sometimes an editor sits on a piece too long and then decides it's no longer timely. (That's happened to me, too.) Sometimes the editor changes her mind about what she wants, or her higher-up does. Sometimes they both do. You can't control any of these scenarios but you can ask that the editor pay the full fee.

While a kill fee provision is created to protect the writer (you get paid at least a little for your work), it shouldn't be used without good reason. If you met the story specs, you should get paid the full fee, and I've argued this point (and know other writers who have as well). Alas, editors almost always fall back on the kill fee clause and refuse to pay the full fee.

Now what? Pitch the piece elsewhere. Don't tell the editor you're querying that it was written and assigned and killed by someone else, possibly one of her competitors (even though you may want to!). Just pitch the piece as if you just came up with the idea, and see if another editor will bite. If so, you may be able to sell the piece you already wrote. If you do have to write a different piece, don't be afraid to pull from your earlier research; when a publication kills a piece, all rights to it revert to you.

Ideally you'll be able to sell the piece to another market and negotiate a better deal for your story. I've had about a dozen stories killed over fifteen years and managed to resell all but one to other markets, which meant that I made up for the lost fee. I even made more money than the original fee for several of the stories, which meant that being killed actually boosted my pay!

Even if you can't resell a story, don't take a piece being killed as a personal attack. If you know you did a good job and met the terms of the assignment, chalk it up to bad luck and consider whether you want to work with that particular editor again.

FORGET PERFECT

As a newbie freelancer, my first assignment for the local newspaper was a profile of the new superintendent of the Coal City School District. It was assigned at 600 words, for $35. I was to interview him about his work background and his plans for Coal City schools in his new position.

I called the new superintendent, set up a time to interview him, and headed out to meet him at his office. I wore a suit left over from my lawyer days and carried a briefcase that included a legal pad, multiple pens, and a tape recorder. On the outside I looked professional and polished. On the inside I was a wreck.

While I'd interviewed sources by phone already, I'd never done an in-person interview before. I wrote out an extensive list of questions so I wouldn't forget anything significant, and the interview went fine. Then I came home to write the piece. I wasn't happy with my first try, so I rewrote it. Then I rewrote it again. And again. I wound up rewriting a 600-word story *seven* times. Finally, I gave up and turned it in. It ran, with two minor edits, in the paper a few days later.

What was my problem? I wanted the piece to be perfect. And there's no such thing. Strive for good, pretty good, or damn good, if you prefer.

I'll tell you something else. I have different standards for different clients. The more I'm being paid, the more time I'm likely to put into a project, and the higher expectation I have of myself. That doesn't mean, however, that I turn in sloppy or unfinished work to my lowest-paying clients. It does mean that if I can do a quick tweak of a story for a reprint market that is going to pay me $50, I'll do it in one pass, without striving for the most stellar lead the way I might with a lucrative feature for a national magazine.

It also means that I keep my client in mind when I'm writing. So, for example, last year I ghostwrote a book for a retired physician, who was a very nice man but was heavy-handed with his edits. He would take what I drafted and completely rewrite it; then I would go back through the new draft, clean it up, and send it back to him for his final review. After the first two chapters, I didn't worry about giving him my "best" work or even close to it. I knew he would rewrite whatever I gave him, so I provided him with serviceable copy that he could chew up and return back to me in an almost unrecognizable form. Then I polished that, and he was happy with my work.

There are times when you want your work to sing. When I write an essay, where every word matters, I spend hours seeking the words that capture the images and emotions I'm trying to convey. I will rewrite until I think it's as perfect as I can make it, at that moment anyway. Then I turn it in.

For most of my work, though, striving for perfection would leave me constantly disappointed, depressed, and broke. You'll be more productive and happier with the quality of your work if you let yourself off of the perfection hook.

So forget perfect. Pretty good or damned good is almost always more than good enough.

42

MAKE YOUR OWN RULES

As a freelancer, you're your own boss. That means you get to make your own rules. I created the 24-Hour-Rule to keep me on target when I started freelancing full-time. A rejection didn't derail me; it just meant that I had twenty-four hours to resub my idea to another market and to pitch a new idea to the editor who had turned me down. [See #11, Employ the 24-Hour Rule.]

Over time, I developed my own guidelines for researching and writing articles. For example, when I started freelancing, I tended to over-research. I'd interview more sources than I actually used in the assigned story, wasting my time and theirs.

Now I use the following "source rule" for stories:

- For a short piece of 300 words or less, I interview and quote one expert or real person, depending on the piece.
- For a story of 300 to 600-700 words, I'll use two sources.
- For a story of 700 to 1,200 words, I'll use three sources.
- For a story of 1,200 to 1,800 words, I'll use four sources.
- For a story of 1,800 to 3,000 words (the longest piece I've written for a publication), I'll use five to eight sources.

While I sometimes interview an extra source or two, my days of interviewing six sources for an 800-word piece (yup, I've done that) are over. If my editor wants something specific, say, a certain number of "real people" quotes, then I'll comply with her request. Otherwise, I stick to my source rule.

I have another guideline for articles I call the "10-percent rule." Imagine that you're polishing that killer 800-word piece (quoting three sources). You've written a scintillating lead, addressed all the relevant points, included insightful quotes, and wrapped the piece up with a strong close. You've pruned every unnecessary phrase and extraneous word, but the story is still running long—at 862 words. What do you do?

In this case, nothing. There's no set standard in the publishing industry, so I decided on the 10-percent rule of thumb. That means a story can be 10 percent over or under the assigned word count without worrying about it.

Of course, I'm going to get as close to the assigned word count as possible. I love turning in a story that's been assigned 1,000 words at 999 or 1,002 or 1,000 words. (Truth is, hitting the exact word count gives me a thrill! Sad, I know.) But that 10 percent bumper means I don't fret if a story is running a little long. (If it's coming in at more than 10 percent over, then it's time for some judicious editing—or a talk with my editor about whether I can take a slightly longer approach to the piece.)

However, in fifteen years, I have never turned in a story that was short on words. First of all, you should always have more than enough words to write any length piece. If you're coming in short, I bet your research is thin or you've missed some aspect of the topic your editor wants you to cover. And you know what? I think an editor may think you didn't do your job if you didn't use every word she's paying for.

Instead of tearing your hair out over an extra 20, or 30, or 90 words, try the 10 percent solution. It may give you the flexibility you need to write a strong piece without sacrificing a critical element in the name of brevity.

I have other rules for my business, too. I follow up on every pitch. I stay in touch with regular clients even if they haven't assigned me any work for a while. I keep track of my invoices so I can get paid in a timely manner.

As a self-employed writer, figure out what writing rules make sense to you (feel free to steal mine), and put them in practice. Having your own guidelines cuts the time you spend worrying about what to do; you simply do it. And that makes you much more efficient both in the short and long term.

PART 3
RELATIONSHIPS: BUILDING AND MAINTAINING CONNECTIONS

Forget the idea of the writer tucked away in her garret; today's successful freelancers know how to create and maintain relationships with people ranging from editors to sources to public relations pros to fellow writers. The good news is that in today's world of social media, it's easier than ever before—but relationship building is more than simply "friending" everyone you know. The secrets in this section will help you learn how to connect and stay connected with the people who will help you succeed as a freelancer.

43

FOLLOW THE PLATINUM RULE

You're no doubt familiar with the Golden Rule—treat others the way you'd like to be treated. Well, when it comes to clients, I'd suggest you up the ante and employ the Platinum Rule—treat them even better than you'd like to be treated.

As a freelancer, you're facing a lot of competition. That means just getting the job done isn't enough. It's the willingness to go beyond what editors and clients require that sets you apart from the freelance pack.

For example, several years ago I interviewed a cake decorator for a trade magazine story. During the course of the interview, she mentioned that the magazine had recently run her photo. Problem was, the person in the picture wasn't her.

Most writers would have shrugged their shoulders, and thought, so what? Instead, I apologized on behalf of the publication, and told her I'd let my editor know. After the interview, I called my editor and told her what had happened, suggesting that we use a photo of the woman and her cakes to accompany my story on cake trends.

My editor agreed and thanked the cake decorator for letting her know about the mistake. I called the decorator back to tell her the magazine would be in touch—and this time, I promised, she would be in the magazine. And she was.

I didn't have to take this extra step—it falls way outside of my job description. But I realized I could probably address what had happened and make the publication (and my editor) look good as well. That helped me build a relationship with an editor who was new to me, and good relationships are critical to success in this business.

How else can you go the extra mile (or two) with a client or editor? Turn stories in early. When you beat your deadline, you give your editor some unexpected breathing room. Trust me, they like this! [See #63, Make every deadline.]

Suggest story ideas—even if you don't write them. I don't do short pieces anymore, but when I come across a new study or press release that would make good FOB material, I pass along the information to my editor. It takes only a few seconds, and shows that I'm thinking of her and trying to make her life a bit easier.

Compliment her. When I receive galleys of a piece or a contributor's copy of the published magazine, I always scan my article for any editorial changes. If the edits strengthened the piece (and they usually do), I'll send a quick note thanking her and telling her the final version looked great. Editors like to receive praise and positive feedback just like we freelancers do.

Keep her up to speed. Several of my editors freelance as well, and I share contact names and industry gossip when I touch base with them. Writers may have access to info through the freelance grapevine that editors don't.

Put yourself in her shoes. Say you're an editor who's turned in a story only to have it slashed to ribbons by your boss. Now you must make your boss, the senior editor, happy. Would you rather work with a writer who complains about revisions or who listens carefully and agrees to revise the story? That's an easy call.

Stop thinking of your clients as merely the people who sign your checks (though that's important too!), and consider how you can make their lives easier. Treat them even better than you'd like to be treated, and it will pay off with loyal customers, and more work in the long run.

44 EMBRACE A PROFESSIONAL PERSONA

I hear from a lot of writers who want to freelance full-time, or who are freelancing on the side but struggling with making enough money or getting enough work. Often one of the things holding them back has little to do with their writing ability. Rather, it's their attitude and the way they approach their writing careers. In short, they're not treating freelancing like a business, but rather as a (hopefully) lucrative hobby.

After fifteen-plus years of full-time freelancing, I can tell you that while attitude *isn't* everything, it *is* a critical factor to your success. It's not only attitude, either; there are other ways to help ensure your success by acting like a professional writer even before you really feel like one, like the following:

DEVELOP RESILIENCE. Let me tell you, not every day of freelancing is all sunshine and roses. Some days stink. Some days I really don't want to freelance anymore, and the idea of returning to a "real" job (complete with paid vacations, sick days, and free coffee!) sounds really attractive. But I also know that these days are part of *any* career, no matter how much you enjoy it.

If you had a bad day at work, you'd chalk it up to just that—a bad day. You wouldn't question your entire career strategy. So don't let a rejection or a harsh note from an editor make you question your ability or desire to freelance. Learn how to shrug it off and keep going.

KEEP REGULAR HOURS. One of the great things about freelancing is that you can set your own hours, whether you freelance full- or part-time. But that flexibility may keep you—or your clients—from taking your work seriously.

I suggest you devote regular time to your freelance business. That doesn't mean you have to punch a metaphorical clock every day at nine A.M. and five P.M., but it does mean that you put consistent time into your work. When I started freelancing, I worked Monday through Friday, starting at about seven A.M. (I'm a morning person) and knocking off in the late afternoon. Today my schedule fluctuates, but I still work Monday through Thursday mornings, eight A.M. to noon, no matter what.

BE RESPONSIVE. We've all worked with editors who take weeks (or longer) to respond, but as a freelancer, you don't have that luxury. You should respond as quickly as possible to phone messages and e-mails from clients and potential clients; that's part of being a professional.

When I worked as a lawyer, my rule was to return all phone calls the day I received them. I can't always be that responsive with *every* e-mail I get, but I do try to reply to all e-mails within two to three days—even if it's just a quick question from a reader or a fellow writer.

TRACK YOUR INCOME. Serious freelancers want to be paid—and hopefully paid well—for their work. To do that, you have to know how much you're making, and where your money comes from. That means keeping track of your assignments and what you're being paid, and following up on unpaid invoices. That's not being a pest—it's being a professional.

PROJECT SUCCESS. Just as successful freelancers must develop resilience, they also must be able to project a successful persona to the world. That means when you attend a writers conference or meet with a potential client, you dress appropriately—say, sporting "business casual" wear, not the jeans and sweatshirt you might wear at home.

But projecting success also includes acting confident, even when you're not. I go through slow work times like any other freelancer, but when I'm contacted by a potential client, I don't say, "thank goodness you're hiring me—I'm broke!" even though I might be thinking that. People want to work with successful people. So, "fake it 'til you make it," and project a confident persona to the world.

CONNECT WITH OTHER WRITERS

While freelancers by necessity work solo most of the time, writers *need* other writers. When you freelance, having writing buddies isn't a bonus. It's a necessity.

While I have and love my nonwriter friends (they're great for serving as sources for stories!), my freelancing friends offer something special:

BUSINESS ADVICE. If I'm struggling to decide whether to take my career in a new direction or take on a particular book project, for example, it helps to bounce it off another freelancer. Many of my freelance friends have been self-employed for as long as I have, or even longer—and they may provide insight that I don't have. They also may help me see that while a particular gig pays well, it's not moving me toward my long-term goals.

AN EDITORIAL EYE. Most of the work I do is relatively easy to write, and I don't have other writers read my stuff before I turn it in. When I write an essay, however, I welcome feedback from friends like Sharon Cindrich, who is a talented essayist. She'll give my piece a read-through and an honest critique—something I can't always get from a nonwriter friend. Her opinion improves my work.

NEW MARKETS. When I was going through a work drought several years ago, my friend Sam Greengard gave me the name of an editor at msnbc.com. I dropped the editor a quick note introducing myself, and a month later, he called to assign me a 700-word piece. I wound up writing several dozen pieces for him. And when my friend Kris Rattini moved to Shanghai years ago, she quit working for her trade magazine clients. I asked if I could contact one of the publications and use her name, and snagged an assignment within a week.

COMMISERATION. As both a freelancer and a mom, it seems like I'm always juggling both roles. I'm fortunate to have not only fellow "mom friends," whose kids know mine, but fellow freelancing parents as well. No one understands the dual role I play—or the guilt I sometimes experience as a working mom—like another freelancer going through the same thing. My closest freelancing friends don't live nearby, but we stay in touch through e-mail and phone calls.

CONNECTIONS. When my editor at Random House called to tell me about a new parenting book project she needed a writer for, I suggested two good friends of mine, Sharon and Kathy Sena. Both happened to be fantastic parenting writers, and out of all of the possible choices, they wound up as the finalists for the book. Neither had written a book before, but Sharon got the contract and has written three other books since then. Being able to help a friend—and my editor—is a wonderful high and helps good things go around.

Developing true friendships takes time and goes beyond commenting on someone's Facebook status. But my freelance friends have done more than introduce me to new markets and help improve my writing, they've helped me celebrate the ups of my career and negotiate the valleys as well. Don't try to go it alone; make an effort to make connections that can turn into lifelong relationships. [See #52, Reach out the right way.] You—and your career—will benefit.

SAY THANK YOU

My mom was (and is) big on thank-you notes. So it's not surprising that when I started freelancing, I decided to send a personal thank-you note to each source I interviewed. By mail. Every time. I've sent hundreds of them over the years, and I'm one of the only writers I know who does this. Yes, it costs me time and money for notes and postage, but it has paid off in ways I wouldn't have anticipated.

First, saying thank you is basic manners. The person you're interviewing is giving you the most valuable thing they have: their time. The cost of a stamp to say that I'm grateful seems like the least I can do. If the interview provided exactly what I needed, I say so. If I really enjoyed speaking with the person, I say so. And if the interview was a dud, well, I can still say I really appreciate the person's time (which I do) and that I'll be in touch with any follow-up questions. Two to three sentences is all that's required, and it takes less than two minutes.

Second, when I call or e-mail with a follow-up question, the person remembers me, which improves my turnaround time. Once I had to call a very busy doctor with a question from my editor. Of course, the editor needed the answer immediately, but the doctor's receptionist told me that he was unavailable for the rest of the day. This was a problem.

"Oh, rats," I said. "Well, can you leave a message for me, then? My name is Kelly James-Enger and I just interviewed him for an article … "

She interrupted me. "Wait, are you the one who sent him that thank you?"

"Um, yes. That's me."

"Hold on," she said. "I'll get him." He was on the line within the minute and gave me the information I needed for my editor.

As a freelancer, you're competing against hundreds of thousands of other writers, many of whom are just as talented as you are, maybe even more so. Figure out a way to make yourself memorable to the people you come in contact with. Sending thank-yous is part of how I run my business, and one of the things I'm known for. I've sent them to clients who have hired me to speak, to agents and editors I've met at conferences, and to people who have referred me to new clients.

I've mailed notes to say congratulations or to tell an author I loved his recent book or just to say I'm thinking of that person. I know I love getting "real" mail and thinking of the reaction of the person getting the note makes my day.

Still not convinced? Well, consider this: Recent research suggests that expressing gratitude does more than please your mom. It boosts your mood and improves your immunity and overall health, at least in the short term.

So, say thank you more often. Better yet, put it in writing.

47

KNOW HOW PERSONAL TO GET

One of the common mistakes freelancers make is in how they treat their clients and editors. Either they don't give them the respect they deserve, or they start thinking of them as their new BFFs. Neither approach works, believe me. You want to take a middle ground.

Two of my biggest rules for client management are "don't make it personal" and "keep it personal." Yup, at first glance they seem contradictory, so let me explain what I mean.

DON'T MAKE IT PERSONAL

My job as a freelancer is to give the client what she wants. Every time—and hopefully the first time out. But sometimes I fail. Maybe I didn't approach the story the way she wanted me to. Or maybe she (or her boss) changed her mind about how the story should be approached. Maybe I didn't do a good job of capturing my ghostwriting client's voice, or maybe he wants me to rework a section of the book because he doesn't like the overall tone.

Regardless of the reason for a revision request or other disagreement, I don't take it personally. Part of writing for money is reworking a piece to meet your client's specifications—and it won't help you to get annoyed or frustrated about it. (I'm talking here about revising a piece once or twice, not working with a client who expects you to rewrite a story or chapter multiple times. That's a different story.)

Listen to your client, and make sure you understand what isn't working for him. Then rewrite the piece to meet his specs. When you're willing to do this—without whining or complaining—you'll help build a positive relationship between the two of you.

...BUT KEEP IT PERSONAL

Wait, didn't I just tell you not to take things personally? This is the flip side of being personal. Here I'm talking about thinking of your client not just as someone who pays you money for your work, but as a *person* as well.

I recently was speaking with an editor I work for who freelances on the side. She mentioned she was having some trouble lining up a couple of "real people" sources for a piece she was doing. I happened to know a couple of women who I thought would work for the story, and I contacted them. Both agreed to be interviewed for the piece—and she appreciated my help.

I don't "friend" *all* of my editors and clients on Facebook, but I do connect with my most important clients online, whether through Facebook, LinkedIn, or Twitter, or a combination of all three. I might comment on their photos or Tweets, and I send holiday cards and gifts to my biggest clients. I genuinely like this group of people (otherwise I wouldn't still be working with them!), and I also know that positive personal relationships with clients help me get more assignments in the long run. It's win-win.

I'm not saying you should expect to be best buds with your clients, but don't be afraid to have some kind of personal relationship with the people you work for. That can help develop a stronger work connection as well.

48 CONDUCT MORE COMPELLING INTERVIEWS

When you interview a source—whether an expert or "real person"—you have a limited amount of time to speak with that person. You can't keep going back to the person as additional questions occur to you—it's unprofessional and will annoy your source! That means you prepare for the interview ahead of time and get as much as you can out of it.

While some freelancers prefer to conduct interviews via e-mail, I almost always conduct them by phone. (I've done a few face-to-face interviews when I'm writing a profile or true-life feature. In those cases, a personal interview is preferable because you can learn a lot about someone by observing his body language and environment.)

Phone interviews take less time and effort for the interviewee (who is doing you a favor by giving you his time, remember), and they're more immediate than an e-mail interview. I've found that e-mail interviews tend to produce canned answers, but I will accommodate sources who request them.

After you've scheduled the interview and confirmed the date, time, and telephone number with your source (remember to double-check time zones and the question of who will initiate the call—sometimes the source will want to call you), prepare for the interview. That may mean doing background research on the subject you're writing about, if you haven't covered it before, or Googling an expert to become more familiar with his expertise. You shouldn't expect anyone to spoon-feed you basic info you can easily locate elsewhere, unless it's to confirm a relevant fact. (For example, I was interviewed by a recent graduate about freelancing, and all but one of his questions was already answered on my website. It was clear that he hadn't done *any* research ahead of time, other than contacting me. That meant he wasted my time and didn't get the best interview from me, either.)

To prevent you from forgetting an essential question, I suggest you write an outline of the questions to cover. In addition, add questions that relate to your topic and include basics like:

- Name, job title, and academic degrees, if applicable;
- Contact information (snail mail address, e-mail, landline, cell phone, fax);
- Book title(s), if applicable;
- Age and other personal information, if applicable. (For example, if you're interviewing moms for a parenting magazine, you may want to ask for the names and ages of their children. If you're interviewing runners for *Runner's World*, you may ask them about their average weekly mileage or marathon personal record.)

When you contact your source, ask if this is still a convenient time for the person to speak with you after you get the pleasantries out of the way. That sets a positive tone for the interview and shows that you appreciate the person's time. It also gives you a chance to reschedule if it's not a good time for her to speak with you. After all, you don't want to conduct an interview with someone who's preoccupied, rushed, or stressed.

If you want to record the interview, ask permission of the source—in some states, it's illegal to tape someone without consent. Otherwise, you can transcribe or jot notes as you go along. I use a headset so I can transcribe as we're speaking, and usually tape-record the interview on a digital recorder. I can then go back and fill in missing info in the transcript afterwards, and it helps me quote sources accurately.

After you get your "basic" questions (the list above) out of the way, continue with the questions that relate to your topic. Make sure that you ask open-ended rather than closed-ended questions for juicier, more compelling quotes. For example, instead of asking, "Is compulsive eating an issue for many women today?" which can be answered with a yes or no, ask "Could you tell me how many women are affected by compulsive eating, and how it impacts them?" See the difference?

Here's another tip to get a great interview from even a reluctant source. You've done your homework, right? So let your source know, in a professional way, like, "Professor, I saw in your CV [curriculum vitae, or professional résumé] that you've done a lot of research on restrained vs. normal eaters, including your recent study on how stress impacts food consumption. I'd like to ask you about how chronic dieters can break free of those habits." By demonstrating that you've educated yourself ahead of time, you'll make a stronger connection with your source.

As you conduct the interview, pay close attention to the subject's answers. Don't worry about getting every word down—that's why you're recording it, so you can fill in any holes later. Look at the interview as a conversation, and don't be afraid to let the interview stray in an unexpected direction. If you find that you're getting way off track, though, let the source finish her thought, and then gently guide her back to the subject with your next question.

After you've finished asking your questions, be sure to give the expert a "softball" question like, "Is there anything I *haven't* asked that you'd like to address, or anything else about the subject you'd like readers to know?" I often get a closing quote or something compelling from that last question.

Depending on the type of source I'm talking to, I may also ask for other suggestions of people to interview—researchers often know who else is working in the field, for example, or a "real person" source may have another person I can speak with.

Finally, close the interview by thanking the expert and telling him that you'll be in touch with any follow-up questions—and send a personal note expressing your appreciation. [See #46, Say thank you.] If you do need to get back in touch with your source in the meantime, chances are that the person will remember your graciousness.

MAKE CLIENTS LOVE YOU

Yesterday I got an e-mail from an editor I worked with six years ago. She wanted to know if I had a story available for reprint on stress-reduction strategies (I have several) and if I were interested in writing original articles for her. Yes, and yes.

Why did she come to me? I'd like to think it's because of my amazing talent as a wordsmith, but it's likely because I e-mailed her a few months ago to touch base and stay on her radar. It worked.

I'm always amazed at the some of the dumb things smart freelancers do to screw up their relationships with the people who make their work and livelihood possible—their clients. Don't make these all-too-common freelance mistakes:

1. **MISS YOUR DEADLINE.** Worse yet, miss your deadline and go AWOL. That happened to an editor of mine. Not only did the writer fail to turn in her assignment, she ignored my editor's (increasingly upset) e-mails and phone calls! If you must blow a deadline, let the editor know in advance, and come up with a plan to get the story done as soon as you can. [See #63, Make every deadline.]

2. **PESTER HIM TOO MUCH.** You already know I believe in following up on queries and LOIs, but I do give potential clients a chance to

respond before I do so. I typically limit my follow-up e-mails to one; two if I've written for the client before. Then I move on.

3. **ARGUE/COMPLAIN/WHINE.** You know what? I'm a hired gun, not an employee—and I'm definitely not the boss. My editor knows her publication and her audience better than I do. That's her job. So if she doesn't think my pitch will work for her magazine, or if she wants me to take another crack at the brochure, I'll honor her decision without arguing over it.

4. **FAIL TO RESPOND.** Yeah, I know that editors take weeks or months to get back to you. But it's different when she's gotten in contact with *you*. You need to reply ASAP—or in twenty-four hours, if possible. No, it's not fair. But that's freelancing.

5. **MAKE IT PERSONAL.** This is similar but not quite the same as #3. Say I ask for more money—$1.50/word—and my editor tells me she can only pay writers $1.25/word. I'm disappointed, but I'm not going to blame her for something that's likely out of her control.

6. **CALL HER.** Editors hate phone calls. They just do. (I do break this rule but only in rare instances, such as when I have a time-sensitive idea.) I limit my phone calls with other clients, too, using them only when necessary.

7. **FORGET WHAT HE WANTS.** Check over your assignment letter (or your notes, if you don't have one) about what the piece was to contain before you turn it in. It looks dumb when you submit a story that's missing a sidebar you agreed to do (and I've done this) or that you went 300 words over word count because your *3* in the 1,300 words you wrote down looked like a *6*.

8. **DO SLOPPY WORK.** Proofread everything before you turn it in. Double-check the spellings of people's names and make sure that you haven't confused *your* and *you're*, and that you're not missing anything. When your stories are riddled with mistakes, you cre-

ate more work for your client—and trust me, he doesn't want or need it.

9. **FORGET TO SAY "THANK YOU."** She probably has dozens, maybe hundreds of writers who would love to work with her. Make sure she knows you appreciate her, even if it's just to say "thanks so much for thinking of me for this assignment."

10. **BAD-MOUTH HER.** Years ago, I was in NYC having coffee with an editor and she told me about a freelancer who had resisted her suggested edits, and then wrote a scathing e-mail to her girlfriend about it. How did the editor know this? Because the freelancer accidentally sent the e-mail to the editor. Yikes! Don't bad-mouth an editor in writing. If she's driving you nuts, pick up the phone to vent to a close friend. Then it won't get back to her.

Editors aren't just paychecks; they're people, too. (Really!) Treat them with respect, avoid driving them crazy, and you'll be rewarded with more work.

CHOOSE RELATIONSHIPS OVER ASSIGNMENTS

You know I do a lot of reslanting, which means I often send the same idea to different markets at the same time. In the publishing business, this is usually called simultaneous submitting or simultaneous submissions.

When I do this, though, I have two rules. First, I make sure I've tweaked the idea for the market I'm pitching. And second, I never simultaneously submit to competing markets.

Let me explain. Say I come up with a story idea on developing a better relationship with your in-laws. I might send that query to a bridal magazine like *Bridal Guide* and then tweak it to apply to marriages of all types (not just new ones) and send it to *Family Circle* at the same time. My logic is that readers of one magazine aren't likely to be reading the other—and the publications aren't competing against each other for readers. (Note that if both pieces are assigned, I'll write two different articles, with different angles, different sources, and different approaches.) However, I won't query the same idea to *Bridal Guide* and *Brides* at the same time—even if it's timely and I want to get an assignment as soon as possible.

Here's why: What happens if editors at both bridal publications want the story? Even if my contracts allow it (and one or both may prohibit me from covering the same topic for a certain time), I guarantee one of them (and possibly both!) is going to be upset when she discovers I'm also covering the topic for her competitor! There goes my relationship with the editor and the magazine ... likely for good.

If two magazines cover the same subjects and seek the same kinds of readers, I consider them competitors. I wouldn't simultaneously submit to *Men's Health* and *Details*, or *O* and *More*, at the same time. But I'd have no problem pitching a piece on middle-aged sex and how to make it better to *Men's Health* and *More* simultaneously.

What if you've got an idea that's highly time-sensitive and you don't want to wait weeks (or longer) to hear back from an editor? I still don't pitch more than one competing market at a time. Instead, I stress the time-sensitive nature of the pitch and either follow up on it right away (within a day or two) by phone or give the editor a tight deadline to respond by. If she doesn't get back to me by that date (which I highlight in the query), I move on to my second-choice market. That keeps my query in play, while still showing respect for the editor at the first publication.

I know some freelancers who take an "open market" approach, simultaneously submitting to competing magazines and selling the idea to the editor who jumps first. I'm not comfortable with that approach. Freelancing isn't about getting assignments. Well, it is, but only in part. At its heart, freelancing is about building relationships with editors.

So, if *Bridal Guide* doesn't want the story, sure, I'll query *Brides* (and no, I won't say, "Hey, so *Bridal Guide* isn't interested...are you?" in my pitch!). If *Self* doesn't want an idea, then I'll take it to *Shape*. But I don't simultaneously submit to competing markets—ever. I'd rather lose some time on a pitch than run the risk of losing an editor—or a market—for good.

51

LEARN TO SAY NO

I admit it. I have a hard time saying no. As a result, I often wind up taking on too much work, only to regret it afterwards. Like most freelancers, I'm always afraid to turn down work—I'd rather say yes to just about everything, which leads to me being overbooked and overwhelmed.

As a former attorney, though, I should know better. As a law student, you study for and take what's called the ethics bar exam, which tests your knowledge of the Code of Professional Responsibility that lawyers swear to uphold. The one thing I remember from the course was this line: *A lawyer is not a bus*. Meaning that if you're uncomfortable working for a client or don't feel that you can adequately represent the person, you don't *have* to take him on—and, in fact, you may be ethically obligated not to. (A bus, on the other hand, stops to let every waiting passenger climb aboard. Get it?)

This axiom applies to *writers* as well. As a freelancer, you don't have to take every project that's offered. Sometimes the gig doesn't offer enough money or the contract terms are terrible or you're already overloaded with work or you don't feel right about the job. Sure, there will be instances where you take on work you're not thrilled about because you need the money. After all, having to do things you don't particularly want to do is part of any job. But if you never say no, you'll lose control over your writing life and have no time for the projects you really want to pursue.

Still, many writers struggle with saying no, especially when they have a relationship with the person doing the asking. Years ago, my dad, who's a dentist, came to me with a great idea. He wanted us to write a book together, on providing better-quality dental care to patients in nursing homes. (Imagine my thrill at the idea of covering this subject!) I had to turn him down.

I felt terrible about it. He's my *dad*! But I knew that the project would take months, it wouldn't produce much (if any) income, and it wasn't a subject I had any interest in. He was disappointed and angry. But if I had taken on the book, it would have severely impacted my ability to make a living.

As a self-employed businessperson, I can't do that. (I would have also been resentful toward him and angry with myself for agreeing to do it, and those are not feelings I want to be embracing for months.)

When I say no, I start with a "thank you," and then give a reason for my refusal, like, "Thank you so much for thinking of me for this project, but I'm afraid I don't have time to take it on right now." Or, "I really appreciate you getting in touch, but I charge at least $4,500 for a book proposal, so unless you can afford that, I won't be able to work with you." You may feel bad temporarily but you'll feel much worse if you take on work that you don't want and then have to actually do it!

Repeat after me: You are a writer, not a bus. Start saying no to the work you don't need and don't want. You won't regret it.

REACH OUT THE RIGHT WAY

Writers need other writers, and this is particularly true for freelancers. I've found the easiest way to connect with another writer is face-to-face, whether it's attending a writers conference, a workshop, or other freelance-oriented event. You either click or you don't, and meeting in person is the fastest way to get to know someone.

But what about connecting through the virtual world? With social media, you can connect through Facebook, LinkedIn, and Twitter, but I've found that e-mailing is the most immediate way to reach another freelancer. E-mail is an excellent tool as long as you avoid these ten mistakes:

DON'T RAMBLE. Don't spill your life story, or even recap the highlights from the last decade. Include a line or two about what you're doing now, writing-wise; long, wordy paragraphs about your entire history or attempts at freelancing overwhelm your recipient and aren't likely to be read.

DON'T E-MAIL "COLD." Don't contact someone without explaining why you're getting in touch. If you have an in, use it. Do you follow the person on Twitter? Did you just read her new novel and enjoyed it? Are you familiar with the person's byline?

When I get an e-mail from a stranger that starts with something like, "I read Six-Figure Freelancing, and loved it," I'm definitely going to continue reading. (If the person is really smart, he writes, "I bought *Six-Figure Freelancing and love it.*" See the difference?)

DON'T ASK FOR TOO MUCH. I'm always happy to answer a quick question, like "What kind of headset do you use?" or "If I haven't received a contract from an editor who assigned a story, what should I do?" or "How much do you charge for reprints?" But when I don't know you from Eve, asking me to read through your book proposal or suggest names of agents for your project or write a book with you is overreaching.

DON'T ASK TO MEET. I just got an e-mail from a writer who wanted to take me to lunch today or tomorrow to "talk about some writing projects." Um, no thanks. Number one, I'm booked today and tomorrow. In fact, I'm booked all week. Number two, you're not offering me a free lunch. You're actually asking me to give up something valuable—several hours of my most productive (and limited) work time. If you e-mail someone, and he wants to meet you in person, he'll suggest it, believe me. Otherwise, assume that your relationship will be through e-mail.

DON'T BE LAZY. I just got an e-mail from a freelancer who had a question about selling reprints. She found my blog and got in touch. If she would have actually *searched* my blog, she would have found the answer to her question. I'll point her in the right direction—she may wind up buying one of my books, after all—but she hasn't made a great first impression on me.

DON'T PESTER. I recently got an e-mail from a freelancer who had contacted me back in September with a question about today's freelance market. She wanted to let me know what had happened with her career in the meantime, and I was delighted to hear from her. But if she was e-mailing me every few days (and believe me, some people have), I'd get annoyed real fast, and eventually would stop responding to her e-mails.

DON'T ASSUME. Like I said, I get lots of e-mails, and I do try to reply to all of them. Don't assume that just because you haven't heard from someone, you've blown it—she's probably just behind on her e-mail. E-mail her again, please. (I just found an e-mail from four weeks ago that I forgot to respond to, which inspired this point.) At the same time, if you've attempted to make contact several times (let's say three or four) and have received no response, it's time to cut bait. Further attempts at contact are akin to stalking.

DON'T GET MAD. I send a personal reply to every *personal* e-mail I get, even if it takes me a few days (or longer) to get to it. But the "spoon-feed-me-please" notes (e.g., "I know you're a freelancer and I want to freelance too, how do I get started?") get a polite, general response suggesting some excellent freelance resources. I can't send a detailed response to every e-mail I get, or I'd have no time left over to actually work! So don't take it personally if you don't get an answer.

DON'T BE SELFISH. When you contact someone, even with a quick question, you're asking for something valuable—their time. So offer something in return, even if it's only to say, "I'd really appreciate your help and will be happy to return the favor." That makes a good impression and makes it more likely for you to get the response you seek. Plus, it's just the right thing to do.

DON'T BE AFRAID. Even the most established freelancer was a newbie at some point, and most experienced writers I know are willing to answer a quick question or two, provided the person follows the guidelines I've suggested. Worst-case scenario, you e-mail someone and never hear back, right? So don't be afraid to try to connect, even if it's just to say that you love the person's work or enjoyed her recent article. You'll feel more a part of the freelance community, especially when you're starting out.

MASTER THE ONE-ON-ONE

As a freelancer, you typically pitch articles (and books) with a written query letter, showcasing your knowledge of the subject and asking for an assignment or book contract. Once you finish it, you e-mail (or less frequently, mail) it off to the editor and wait for a response. Easy enough.

But what happens when you have a one-on-one meeting with an agent or editor at a writers conference or other event? Face-to-face meetings offer a host of advantages over a written pitch, but most writers go cold at the idea of meeting with an editor across a table. Keep a few strategies in mind and you'll shine at one-on-ones whether you're meeting with an editor, agent, or potential client, like a corporate communications director.

DO YOUR HOMEWORK

Do some research ahead of time so you can make the most of your one-on-one session. When pitching a magazine editor via query, you might just glance at a copy of the publication to determine where your article might fit. Here you want to demonstrate more in-depth knowledge of his publication.

The same is true when meeting with an agent or book editor. Most writers focus on selling their work, not on the needs and interests of the editor or agent. When you demonstrate that you've done some background on the person (e.g., "So, I noticed that you sold *Lincoln Lied*, a history book, several months ago. Are you still looking for historical nonfiction?"), the agent or editor is going to be much more interested in hearing your pitch.

Today, every publisher and agent has a website, so there is no excuse for not doing your homework. Yet at one-on-ones, both editors and agents are routinely pitched books that they would never acquire or represent. That's a huge waste of your time—and theirs.

And if you're meeting with a prospective client, you should go in with some knowledge of its business. When I met with the director of marketing for a nonprofit, I'd visited the website of the organization and knew about its mission and work. That kind of preparation set the tone for my "interview" and led to a lucrative project just a week later.

PLAN TO TALK—AND LISTEN

A query letter or letter of introduction is a one-way exchange. A one-on-one meeting gives you the opportunity to not only pitch, but to listen and respond to what the editor says. It's also an opportunity to get the insider's track on the publication. Is the magazine going to be moving in a new direction? Becoming more service oriented? Is it looking to broaden its audience?

If you're meeting with a literary agent, ask who his "dream client" is. Does he have a certain type of book he likes to represent? What are his favorite publishers or editors, and why? What does he like to see in a book proposal?

With a book editor, you might ask about her favorite books—not only the ones she's read, but the one's she's edited. Is she looking for books in areas she already covers or does she plan to expand into other topics? How hands-on is she as an editor? What are her personal pet peeves with authors ... or what do her favorite authors have in common? You can garner a lot of knowledge from simple questions.

If you're meeting with a corporate communications manager or other potential client, you'll want to learn more about the company and what she is looking for. How often does she hire freelancers? For what types of projects? What style book (i.e., Chicago or Associated Press) does the company use? Does the company have its own style sheet (i.e., preferential spellings and uses of commonly used terms)? Do freelancers work on-site or at home?

HAVE BACK-POCKET IDEAS

When you pitch an idea via query, you may wait weeks (or months!) for a response. With a one-on-one meeting, you're likely to get a response immediately—even if it's, "That sounds interesting. Why don't you send me a query after the conference?" That's good news. But what if you offer an idea and the editor passes. Then what?

Sure, you can talk to the editor about her likes and dislikes. But for meetings with magazine editors, I suggest having more than one idea to pitch. At one-on-one meetings with magazine editors, I always have at least five compelling article ideas to discuss. I start with what I think is my strongest idea and go from there.

If you're meeting with an agent, this is trickier. Let's say you're pitching your nonfiction book and the agent isn't interested. Then what? No one expects you to have two completely different book projects to pitch. But instead of saying, "Okay, thanks," and ending the session, why not get more information? Ask her why she's not interested in your project or if she has any suggestions about how you can make it more marketable. Don't argue the merits of your book or try to talk her into taking you on. If asked politely, however, she may give you some advice that you can use to improve your proposal or novel—and garner another agent's interest.

The same goes with a book editor meeting. If you have only one idea to pitch and the editor isn't interested in your book, ask him for his opinion about your book and its strengths and weaknesses. Once he says no, that does mean no. But he may have ideas and insight for you to take home.

With a potential business client, you want to spend some time exploring what the client wants and needs. Then you can demonstrate how you can meet those needs. Bring your portfolio or samples of your written work. Ideally your samples will be as close to the type of work he's looking to hire out. (In other words, if he's looking for a writer of newsletter articles, you bring newsletters you've written. If you don't have anything that matches exactly, just bring your portfolio and play up your experience with the subject matter, if appropriate, and your ability to create different types of written pieces.)

PRACTICE YOUR PITCH

Finally, because these meetings are typically short, you'll want to practice your pitch ahead of time. If you're pitching a magazine article, use the lead you'd write in a query. If you're pitching a book, however, you want to spend some time developing your "elevator speech" ahead of time.

Your elevator speech is a compelling paragraph about your book and its audience. It's a condensed version of your book, playing up its most interesting and marketable elements. If you stepped into an elevator and had less than a minute to impress your dream agent, how would you wow him? Here's an example: "There are millions of people interested in freelance writing, but most of them have no idea about how to succeed in the business. As a successful freelancer for fifteen years, my book, *Writer for Hire,* will provide both new and experienced writers with the advice they need to launch successful careers."

The elevator speech is the opener, but you should be prepared to demonstrate your platform, or your knowledge, experience, media connections and ability to sell your book after you catch her attention.

Remember to thank anyone you meet for taking the time to talk with you. If you have interest from an editor or agent, follow up promptly (within a week of the conference, if possible) to strike while she will remember your name and idea. Your face-to-face meeting may open the door for you, but following up will help seal the deal.

NAME YOUR WHALES

You may have heard of the 80/20 rule in business, which says that 80 percent of your income (and your work) comes from 20 percent of your clients. In the gaming industry, high rollers are called "whales," and casino staffers do everything possible to encourage them to spend time and money at their casinos.

Do you know who your whales are? The only way to be sure is to (eek!) do some math.

The end of the year is the perfect time to take a closer look at your income. Every quarter, I add up my gross income, but the last quarter of the year I take it a step further, and divide it by client. Then I categorize my income into groups—like money from original magazine articles; money from my own books; money from ghostwriting and co-authoring clients' books; money from reprints; and money from teaching and speaking.

Totaling these figures tells me where my money is coming from and what types of work have been the most lucrative for me. It also helps me set my goals for the coming year. I might decide to increase the percentage of income I receive from books, for example, or double the amount I make from reprints, which are a relatively easy way to make extra money.

You can do the same thing quite easily. At the end of the year (or any other time you want), list your clients and add up what each has paid you this year. Then determine what types of work you've been paid for in the past year. The categories you use will depend on the nature of freelance work you perform. If you write for magazines, perform PR work for nonprofits, and copywrite for corporations, for example, then add up the income you've made for each type.

Adding up your income and where it came from is a critical first step. With this information, you can set more specific, realistic career goals for the coming year, focusing on what areas of your business are promising. You'll also identify your whales—the clients who provide you with the most work and money. Those are the ones you want to continue to work for. It's much more efficient to do a lot of work for a small number of clients than it is to do a small amount of work for many clients. This seems obvious, but a lot of freelancers don't take the time to determine who their most valuable clients are, and then focus more time and energy on them.

Your mileage, of course, may vary. If you write books or ghostwrite, you may have more one-shots, or clients you only write for once. In this case, you may have different whales each year, but I still suggest you stay in touch with each; they're a source of referrals and possibly more work in the future.

Then go a step further and consider cutting ties with clients who aren't worth the time and effort. If you're writing for more than ten clients a year, chances are that there is some dead weight—let's call them remoras—on your client list. Maybe you've been writing for a client for years but your hourly rate isn't all that great. Or maybe the client's PIA (that's my term for Pain In the…) factor has grown so high you'd like to say goodbye. [See #64, Fire clients.] Every client you work for involves opportunity cost, and if you never get rid of your remoras, you may be losing out on more lucrative ones.

Make it an annual goal to determine not just your income, but where it comes from. When you know who your whales are, you can make sure they get the attention they deserve.

55

ATTEND A CONFERENCE (OR TWO)

A writers conference saved my career.

I'd only been freelancing for eleven months when I attended a Magazine Writers & Editors/One-on-One, a Chicago-based conference for magazine freelancers. I was finding that freelancing was a lot tougher than I'd expected and was considering looking for another job to support my fledgling career. I thought the conference might be a chance to meet some editors and hopefully get some more assignments.

For entry into the competitive conference, you had to apply with at least three clips from national magazines. At the time, I had exactly that many. I sent in my application and clips without pointing out that they were also my only clips, and crossed my fingers.

Well, I got in. The first day, I turned to the woman sitting next to me to introduce myself. "What kind of work do you do?" I asked politely. She rattled off a list of magazines that I'd only dreamt of writing for. Oh, and she was a book author as well. I gulped and turned to the woman on my left. She had been a full-time editor for a big publisher for more than fifteen years and wrote travel articles for national mags.

I sat there, thinking of my total of three clips and vowed not to initiate conversation with anyone else. I even thought about sneaking out and going home. Later, at the get-to-know-you cocktail party, I came out of my corner and introduced myself to a woman who looked like I felt. We bonded immediately and fourteen years later, Kris and I are still close friends.

I didn't just make a writing buddy at the conference. I found a home. I'd never met a freelancer, let alone a successful one, before I'd quit to write full-time. Now I was surrounded by them. I eavesdropped on conversations. I watched how they chatted with their colleagues, and how they talked matter-of-factly about contracts and assignments and juggling work and families.

Being around dozens of smart, articulate, enthusiastic writers boosted my confidence. These men and women didn't seem all that different from me, even if they were further along in their careers. If they were doing it, why couldn't I?

That conference led to multiple assignments from one of the editors there, which repaid my investment many times over. Its true value is impossible to calculate. In just three days, I was transformed from someone who had been freelancing on little more than a whim to someone who decided to take charge of my business and commit to it for the long haul.

Interacting and networking with other writers is only one of the reasons I find writers conferences so valuable. Conferences also let you hear from other pros in the publishing trenches—book and magazine editors, literary agents, and other freelancers—about what is happening in the industry today. You learn what editors like and are looking for from pitches or book proposals, what rates different markets are paying, and how authors are harnessing social media to build their platforms. Even if I've left a conference without obtaining a specific assignment, I've always found attending them worthwhile.

Sadly, One-on-One is no longer around. But every year I try to attend ASJA's annual conference in New York City at the end of April. It's aimed at freelancers who write nonfiction books, articles, blogs, you name it, and features dozens of editors and agents. It's the best networking I get all year long, and I recommend it to serious freelancers.

Look for a conference that covers topics of interest to you; you can search Shawguides.com for conferences by topic, location, and time of year. I've attended and spoken at dozens of events; some of my favorites besides ASJA include Willamette Writers annual conference (Portland, Oregon), the annual Writers Institute (Madison, Wisconsin), and Writers' Fest (Milwaukee, Wisconsin).

Before the conference, take a look at the schedule and decide which panels you'll attend. (Panel turns out to be a dud? Don't feel bad about leaving to check out another one.) Sign up for one-on-one appointments if they're available. Even if you're a wallflower by nature, introduce yourself to the people around you. Swap business cards and contact information.

Take careful notes at panels you attend. Pay attention to what editors and clients say they want, and plan to pitch or follow up with people during the week afterwards. (Most freelancers won't bother, so you'll stand out.)

And finally, let yourself soak up the energy of the freelancers around you and be open to the information that's shared. You'll come away with new ideas, new perspectives, new contacts, and new enthusiasm for your chosen career.

56

AVOID EXPLOSIVES AND WAIFS

Early in my career, I connected with another writer through an e-mail list for freelancers. We met a few times for coffee or lunch. She and I didn't really click, but I was so desperate for some writing companionship, I pursued the relationship. Today I wouldn't bother because I've gotten more selective about whom I connect with—and I have less time to do that connecting.

As a writer, you spend much of your working life alone, but the relationships you have with clients, editors, sources, and other writers play a critical role in your success. Freelance long enough, though, and you'll find that not every fellow writer becomes your BFF (that's best friend forever for those who don't know).

Fact is, every profession has its archetypes, some more destructive than others. Watch out for these writers:

- **THE EXPLOSIVE.** The Explosive is just that—a ticking bomb that's easily triggered. Explosives are always ranting about something. Explosives have lots of energy they could channel into their writing (and sometimes they do), but they devote just as much of it to justifiable (to them) rages. Steer clear of Explosives. If you get too close, you may find you're the target of her latest diatribe.

- **THE STAR.** It's all about her. I had coffee with a freelancer in New York, and she spent ninety minutes talking about her latest book series, her new novel, her popularity, her legion of Twitter followers (this was before I'd ever sent a Tweet, of course), and her general fabulousness. I sat there, nearly mute, as she ran over my every attempt to enter the conversation with more than a nod or a "wow, that's great." By the time it was time to leave (I'd been glancing at my watch for a good fifteen minutes), she said, "Gosh, we haven't even had a chance to talk about you! We'll have to get together again soon!" Thanks, but no. The Star has no interest in a real relationship—she's only looking for someone to reflect her glory back at her.

- **THE WHINER.** While the Explosive is filled with rage, the Whiner can't summon enough energy for anger. So he whines instead: about the unfairness of contracts, about editors who expect revisions, about plummeting advances, about pretty much everything. This is the kind of person who, if he won the lottery, would gripe about the taxes. No matter how successful he becomes (and he probably won't, thanks to his attitude), he'll never be happy—or much fun to be around.
- **THE WEIRDO.** The Weirdo stands a little too close when you meet him in person, or he stares at you without saying much. He IMs you on Facebook when the only reason you Friended him is because you share eighty-nine mutual friends, and then asks you odd, intimate questions that have nothing to with freelancing. (I speak from experience.) Time to cut bait—and be more choosy about whom you connect with on social media. The Weirdo may be perfectly nice, but do you want to connect with someone who makes you uncomfortable?
- **THE WAIF.** She wants so much to freelance, and just needs a little help from you. Then a little more. Then a little more. Regardless of age or experience, the Waif is an emotional vampire who will always want and expect more than you can give. You feel sorry for her at first but understand that the time you devote to her takes time away from your own work.
- **THE USER.** The User only reaches out because you have something she wants. Once she's gotten it, you won't hear anything from her. I got the brush-off at a conference from a freelancer much further

> along in his career than I was—until he realized who my agent was and wanted to talk to me about getting her to represent him. Then he couldn't have been more gracious. Strange, huh? I'm all for give-and-take with other fellow freelancers, but there are writers who only connect with you for their own reasons and then disappear when you ask that the favor be returned. You'll figure out pretty quickly who falls into this category.

Bottom line? Don't waste your time on writers who are only about themselves. Most of the freelancers I've met online and in person are professional and personable, and want to support other writers. As you gain experience, you'll find plenty of them, and gain freelancing colleagues and freelancing friends.

MAKE SOURCES LOVE YOU

As a freelancer, you spend a significant amount of time conducting research to learn and master the subjects that you write about. In addition to background research, which can be conducted on your own, you'll conduct interviews with sources.

Most writers look at every interview as a means to an end. You find a potential source, line up an interview, conduct it, thank the person (I hope), and move on. [See #48, Conduct more compelling interviews.]

That's shortsighted in my opinion. Treat your sources with respect and appreciation, and you'll get more than the information and quotes you need for your article or blog post. You'll build a database of sources for the future and build your network as well.

Here are five simple ways to make your sources love you:

GIVE THEM THE HEADS-UP. When I contact a source to arrange an interview, I tell her a little bit about the piece I'm writing and what I plan to ask. For example, I might say, "I'm writing a piece on the benefits of risk-taking and would like to ask you about the psychology of risk-taking—like why some people are more willing to take risks and the benefits of trying something that scares you. And if you could offer some advice for readers about how to take more risks in their life, that would be great."

Get it? If I asked you right now to tell me the six secrets to a happy relationship, you'd likely stammer out something that may or may not be useful. But if I tell you I'm going to call you tomorrow night at seven P.M. Central Time to ask you the same question, you'll have a chance to prepare. You'll be able to give me what I need for the story and offer me more interesting quotes, too.

Keep in mind that I'm not an investigative reporter. I'm not trying to catch people off-guard or trick them into saying something they'll regret. I want useful information and compelling quotes, and I'm more likely to get them when my sources have a chance to prepare ahead of time. That's why I give them an idea of what to expect.

SHOW RESPECT. If you line up an interview for 10:15 A.M., call at 10:15 A.M. I can't tell you how many of my sources are surprised when I call as scheduled. Doing what you promised starts the interview off on a positive note. If you're running late, let the source know at least as soon as you know that you can't make the prearranged time. Then reschedule, even if it's only by pushing the time back by fifteen minutes. Crises arise—everyone understands that. It's how you handle them that is important.

And before you launch into your questions, make sure you ask if this time still works for the person. Let the person reschedule if necessary. Again, you want the person focused on you, not worried about making a meeting or picking up his child from basketball practice.

SHOW YOUR HAND. My friend Kristin Baird Rattini writes a lot of celebrity profiles, which means she's speaking with people who have been interviewed hundreds of times. She doesn't want the same canned responses that celebs tend to give, so she does a lot of background research before her interview.

"Before I interview a celebrity, I read as many of their previous interviews I can find. That research helps me avoid questions they've been asked over and over—and to which they've given the same rote response over and over," says Rattini, a veteran freelancer based in St. Louis and a frequent contributor to *American Way* and *National Geographic Kids,* among other publications. "If it's an unavoidable question, I make sure to phrase it differently enough to guarantee an original reply. In fact, during my interviews I'll often say, 'You've said in previous interviews' or 'You stated on *The Tonight Show* (or in *Elle*, on *Conan*, etc.),' which lets me do two things: 1) build on and elaborate on the previous question/response, and 2) telegraph to them that I've done my homework."

Rattini makes sure that her sources know early on in the interview that she has studied their work and educated herself about their background. "For a recent interview with Jane Lynch, I had to ask the rote question about 'So, how did you feel about how Season 2 of *Glee* ended for Sue Sylvester?' But in doing so I cited the exact name of the new political party her character intended to create. Lynch said, 'Wow, good for you for knowing that!'" says Rattini. "That was a detail for which I purposely went back to my DVR copy of that particular episode so I could get it right. I also cited specific, detailed anecdotes from her new memoir, nearly word for word. She commented, 'You really did your research!' I am confident that my research earned her respect and therefore resulted in far richer quotes than she might have given otherwise."

While I don't do many celebrity interviews, I use Rattini's approach with experts and "real people" sources. Say I'm speaking with an anecdotal source whose name was given to me by a friend. I'll start out by saying something like, "I know you're good friends with Katie, and she told me that even with four kids you find time to exercise regularly. That's what I'd like to ask you about—not just how you do it, but what advice you have for other parents." I don't take as much time to prepare for an interview with an anecdotal source as I do with an expert or "name," but I let both types of sources know I appreciate their time.

TELL THEM WHEN THEY'RE QUOTED. As a freelancing expert and book author, I've been interviewed dozens of times over the years, yet I rarely know when the article runs. Writers who tell me when I'm quoted in print or online get big points from me. I don't care whether you're interviewing an expert source or a real person, they appreciate knowing when they've been quoted.

In the event that I don't quote the source directly in the piece (or the editor cut a quote or source, which happens frequently), I still notify the source with a quick e-mail, saying something like, "I just wanted to let you know that my piece on workout strategies for busy moms is out in the latest issue of *Chicago Parent*. Due to the number of sources I interviewed, I wasn't able to use a direct quote from you in the story, but I truly appreciate your time and help with the piece, and hope you enjoy it."

EXPLAIN WHAT YOU CAN AND CAN'T DO. As a freelancer, I have no say in when (or even if) a story runs, what the story will eventually look like, and what sources make it into the piece. So when I'm speaking with a source and the interview is turning out to be a dud, I may wrap up the interview with language like, "Thanks so much for speaking with me for this piece. I'm interviewing a lot of sources for the story, so I'm not sure who will wind up being quoted in the piece, but regardless I'll let you know when the story runs."

When I say something like this, I already know that I'm probably not going to use the person in the piece. In other cases, my editor will cut a source during the editing process. If that's what happens, I'll explain it to the source and that it has nothing to do with him or her and that I'll keep the person's contact information on file. Often I'll wind up using that source for another piece.

Finally, tell every source you interview that you appreciate his time, or better yet, send a personal thank-you note. [See #46, Say thank you.] That single step will help sources remember you and help you create relationships with different types of sources you can use for other work in the future.

GATHER—AND SHARE—INFORMATION

Years ago, a member of ASJA posted on the group's members-only bulletin board about the recent success she'd had selling reprints of some of her work to an international syndication group—and shared the name and the e-mail of her contact person there. I got in touch and promptly sold nearly $3,000 worth of reprints to several Australian and Asian magazines I hadn't even known existed.

I sent the writer a personal thank-you note (big surprise, huh?) and included the names and e-mails of several of my best reprint markets. I told her I thought it was the least I could do for being so generous. She replied to my note, thanking me for sharing some of my reprint markets. We've stayed in touch and swapped reprint markets since then—and we've both made money as a result.

I'm known for being willing to talk about money. For example, I've shared in articles and books, and on my blog, how much I make per year and what I'm paid for different types of work from books to articles to speaking gigs. (One of the reasons I joined ASJA was for access to its paycheck database, where writers anonymously report what publishers pay for different types of work. It's an invaluable resource.)

Yet I know some writers who won't talk money, whether it's the amount they were paid for a book advance or what they gross per year. I don't get that. To me, the amount of money you're paid has little to do with your value as a writer or a person. It's only an indicator of the value the publisher or client placed on your work. And as freelancers, the more we share with each other, the more power each of us has.

That said, even I don't share *everything*. If you were to e-mail me and ask me how much a certain market pays me, I'll tell you. But if you were to ask me for all of my editors' names and contact info? Um, I don't think so—that's overstepping.

So don't be afraid to ask another writer for information. Worst-case scenario, the writer says no, and you're no better off than you were. E-mail someone you have some connection with, whether online or in person, and ask for one piece of information, whether it's the name of an editor at a particular magazine or how much a market pays, and offer something valuable in return.

Here's an example: "Hi, Gina, I know your name from Freelance Success [an online members-only freelance bulletin board], and noticed that you've written for *Women's Health*. I have several ideas I'd like to pitch there—would you mind if I ask the name of the editor you work with there? I've written for *Shape* and would be happy to give you my editor's name if you're interested. Thank you so much for considering this."

See how easy it is? Ask for something reasonable, offer something in return, and be sure to say thank you. You can start creating your own "knowledge base" of market and pay information that will benefit you in the future.

PART 4
MANAGEMENT: RUNNING YOUR BUSINESS LIKE A BUSINESS

As a freelancer, you're self-employed and that means one of the hats you wear is "office manager." Most writers don't enjoy this aspect of freelancing, but comporting yourself like a successful businessperson is essential to your success. Treating your writing like a business includes everything from asking—and getting—more money, deciphering freelance contracts, collecting outstanding invoices, and tracking your business expenses, among other things. The secrets in this section will help you think, and act, like a successful businessperson, who happens to be a writer.

59

ASK FOR MORE

Nothing strikes fear into the heart of a freelancer like asking for more money. What do you say? How do you ask for more without offending a client—or worse, having him pull the assignment from you?

If you've never tried to negotiate for more money, it's normal to be nervous. I was a lawyer in my former life and it still took me more than thirteen months of full-time freelancing before I summoned up the courage to ask for more than I was offered. But if you never ask, you'll never get it.

Asking for more money is as simple as "TEA." Use this three-step method to ask for more money, and you're likely to get it:

1. **THANK.** When you're offered an assignment, express your appreciation. Let the client know you're excited about or looking forward to working with him (e.g., "Thanks so much for thinking of me … " or "I'm glad you want to assign me this piece.")

2. **EXPLAIN.** Now give a reason (or more than one) why you're asking for more money. The way you make your case will depend on the assignment, but I've used the following reasons to ask for more:

    - A tight (or extremely tight) deadline (e.g., "I'm happy to take this on, but the deadline means I'm going to have to work nights to meet it … ").
    - An all-rights contract that the editor won't budge on (e.g., "I realize you can't change the contract, but this prevents me from ever reselling the story in the future and as a freelancer, I rely on reprints to fund my 401(k) … ")
    - A story that requires a lot of legwork (e.g., "Hey, we both know how hard it can be to find 'real people' sources for this kind of story … ").
    - An assignment that requires a certain level of expertise or experience (e.g., "You know that I've been doing health writing for more than a decade, and I'm happy to do all the background research this story will require … " or "I've written more than a dozen book proposals that have sold, so you know I can write a proposal that will capture an editor's attention … ".
    - A market that I've written for before (e.g., "You already know I'm going to do a great job for you … ").

3. **ASK.** It's that simple. After you've expressed enthusiasm for and appreciation of the assignment, and after you have stated your case, ask the editor if she can "do better." (You don't have to say, "Pay me more, dude!" even if that's what you're thinking.) The way you phrase it will vary, so use language you're comfortable with. I find

it helps to have some scripts at my disposal. Here are some sample scripts, using the above scenarios:

- Tight deadline script: "Thanks so much for thinking of me for this story. I'm happy to take this on, but the deadline means I'm going to have to work some nights to meet it. Considering that, can you boost your rate a bit?"
- All-rights contract script: "I realize you can't change the contract, but this prevents me from ever reselling the story in the future, and as a freelancer, I rely on reprints to fund my 401(k)—I don't have a pension plan. Keeping that in mind, could you do better moneywise?"
- Legwork-heavy story: "Hey, we both know how hard it can be to find 'real people' sources for this kind of story ... it can take days just to find the right person! Can you do better than $1/word for that kind of legwork?"
- Complex or complicated assignment script: "You know that I've been doing health writing for more than a decade, and I'm happy to do all the background research this story will require, but this is a story not everyone could write. Can you do better moneywise to reflect my experience?"
- Regular market script: "You know me and my work, and you know I'm going to do a great job for you and turn the story in before deadline. Could we talk about me getting a raise?"

Thank. Explain. Ask. It's that simple. Try TEA before you say yes, and there's a good chance your client will offer more money. And if he doesn't, and you still want the assignment, be gracious. Say something like, "Well, it never hurts to ask, and I'm really looking forward to working with you on this piece. Maybe in the future we can revisit what I'm paid." This keeps your relationship on a positive note.

And if the offer isn't enough for you to take on the piece, you can always say no—graciously. If the terms change, maybe you'll eventually be able to say yes.

60

KNOW YOUR BOOK PUBLISHING OPTIONS

If you've been freelancing for a while, perhaps specializing in a subject or two, you may consider branching out into books. Twenty years ago, if you had a book to publish, you had two basic options—sell it to a traditional publisher, or publish your work yourself with a vanity press. Not so today. If becoming an author is on your horizon, you have more choices than ever before, so you should be aware of the pros and cons of each.

When you picture publishing a book, you're probably thinking of the traditional model. Whether a big publisher like Random House, a smaller publisher that publishes a few titles a year, or an academic publisher that typically produces books in a limited subject area, a traditional publishing house acquires the rights to publish your manuscript. They usually pay an advance (technically an "advance against royalties," a percentage you're paid for each book sale as its author), although advances have shrunk over the last couple of years.

The publisher acquires the rights to your book, and you write it. The publisher then is responsible for editing, layout, printing, and distribution. (In theory, the publisher also assists with publicity and promotion. However, unless you're a big-name author like Patricia Cornwell or Tom Clancy, the fact is that the author carries the lion's share of the promotional burden.)

When I entered the world of books eleven years ago, I chose to take the traditional route for several reasons. Number one, I wanted (and needed) the advance up-front so I could afford to take time to write the book. Second, I didn't have time or the desire to be wholly responsible for the layout, printing, and publishing of my manuscript. Third, I'd seen a lot of poorly produced self-published books that turned me off to the concept.

Things have changed a lot in the last decade, though. According to *Publishers Weekly*, self-publishing and print on demand, or POD, books accounted for 63 percent of all books printed in 2009 and that ratio is continuing to increase. Why? First, POD has no barriers to entry. If you want to publish a book, you can. You needn't sell it to a traditional publisher first.

If you choose to go POD, you can also get your book in print much more quickly—in as little as two or three months. Compare this to traditional publishers, which typically work at least twelve months ahead of a publication date.

Of course, throwing the doors open to all means that some POD books are poorly (or not at all) edited. Skimping on editing, layout, and design means that some self-published books look unprofessional, or worse, sloppy. A bigger issue for POD and other self-published titles is distribution—or lack of it. POD companies don't have the distribution network that traditional publishers have, so your book isn't likely to be sold through bookstores or to libraries (unless you can create interest in the book on your own).

There are several dozen POD companies including AuthorHouse, Lulu, and CreateSpace. Their packages vary, but on average you can expect to spend between $400 and $700 to get your book into print. Compare their offerings, and look for a company that charges a low fee for formatting and producing your book, and will handle online orders and place your book in all online databases for retail and library sales. Some POD companies charge higher fees but offer additional marketing and promotion packages and distribution. However, read any contract you sign carefully—you may wind up spending a lot of money for work you could do (and probably will have to do) yourself.

The newcomer to the scene and the fastest growing option is the e-book. Traditional publishers are now putting out both print and electronic versions of books, and POD companies offer the option for you to do the same. Or you can choose to publish your book solely as an e-book. If you take the time to format your manuscript, you can upload your file to a company like Smashwords for no charge. E-books are typically priced lower than print books (the most popular price at the moment for self-published e-books appears to be $2.99, while traditionally-published e-books are often priced at $9.99-12.99), and they offer the fastest way to get your book published.

There's one final option, too, and that's "true" self-publishing. As a self-publisher, you're in control of all the details. You design the interior and exterior of the book (or hire it done), hire a printer, market, distribute, you name it. You can make a lot more per-book when you self-publish, but the amount of time involved prevents most would-be authors from pursuing this option for a print book. However, as e-books continue to gain popularity and readers, more authors are choosing virtual books over print—and that trend is likely to continue.

Think about your goals for your book, and your overall goals as an author, to determine the best option for you. Many authors want the distribution and support of a traditional publisher, not to mention an advance, even if it's a small one. Others don't want to wait a year or more to get their book into print (assuming they can sell it to a traditional publisher) and choose to go POD or publish an e-book. Neither of the latter pays an advance, but you'll make money on every book that sells. If you're committed to marketing your book (and I hope you are), those sales can become a steady income stream for you as an author.

FORGET PER-WORD RATES

I've seen both new and experienced freelancers get hung up on what they make per *word*.

To which I say—who cares? I only care about what I make per *hour*.

Per-word rates are the norm in the magazine, newspaper, and online world. This figure, multiplied by word count, tells you how much you'll make for writing a particular story. But it may not tell you whether it's worth it to take it on. The real question is how much time the story will take—the assignment amount divided by the number of hours you put into it gives you your hourly rate for the piece.

Knowing how much time an article (or any other project, for that matter) will take gives you a concrete idea of the return on your time. And those $1/word and up assignments can be mighty misleading. Sure, it's a bigger check than writing for a market that pays a lower per-word rate. But are you really making more money?

For example, let's say I do a 1,000-word story for a national magazine that pays $1.50/word. Fair enough—I'm getting paid $1,500 for my work. But what happens if between researching and writing the query, writing an outline (per my editor's request), researching the article, finding sources, doing interviews, transcribing interviews, writing the piece, turning in the piece, revising the piece (per my editor's request), finding new sources (per my editor's request), interviewing those sources, turning in the final revision, submitting my backup material, answering additional questions from the editor (say, nine months later ... yes, it happens), I've put twenty-five hours into my story? That means I've made $60/hour on that story.

Not bad, but here's the thing—compare that to a 1,000-word piece on the same topic for a smaller magazine that pays only $0.35/word. I know the editor and my query consists of a brief paragraph. The story requires some background research and several interviews, and takes me a total of five hours to write. (No revisions requested! Yay!) That's a total of $350, for five hours' worth of work—or $70/hour.

At first glance, the $1,500 piece looks like a better assignment—and it is a bigger check. But my experience has been that national markets (and I've written for more than fifty of them) expect a lot more work from you to earn that higher rate. In many cases, I've found that regional magazines, trade publications, and specialty magazines actually pay better per-hour than their national counterparts. And that makes them worthwhile markets for me.

Don't be sucked in by a high per-word rate, or scoff at a low one—until you know what the real figure you should focus on is. And that figure is your per-hour rate.

PLAN ON PAYMENT

The type of freelance work you do will vary, but your ideal client pays promptly (and well) for your work. So, let's take a look at when you can expect to be paid—and help ensure that you get those checks promptly.

As the economy has tanked, your chance of experiencing "slow-pay" (or worse, "no-pay") clients has increased. You need to know what's typical so you can keep tabs on your accounts receivable and follow up on outstanding invoices, if necessary. [See #67, Collect every check.]

In the past, national magazines paid within about four weeks of accepting a story; today, it's more like six to eight weeks. I've found that trade and regional magazines, which have fewer levels of bureaucracy, tend to pay more quickly. Business clients generally pay within two to four weeks of receiving an invoice. If you're working for a book publisher, your contract will spell out when you'll be paid and how much (for instance, you may get half of your advance upon signing the deal), but many publishers are taking weeks, even months, to actually cut those checks.

When writing for magazines, newspapers, or websites, you want payment "on acceptance," not payment "on publication." With the former, when an editor signs off on your story, she'll either ask you for an invoice or put payment through by requesting that the accounts payable department cut you a check—or make a deposit in your bank account if you've set that up with the publisher. (More publishers are offering this option, which means you get your money faster. I choose it whenever I can.)

With payment on publication, or payment on pub, however, you're issued a check about the time the story runs. The problem? Who knows when exactly that will be? If you've written the story, you've fulfilled the terms of your agreement. Why should you be penalized because a market decides not to run your piece, or even folds before the piece is published?

Some smaller markets do insist on payment on publication. For example, many of my reprint markets pay on pub. I still sell to them because the work (the actual research for and writing of the story) has already been completed, and the checks are small, typically $40 to $150. Failing to receive one isn't going to make or break my month.

Consider, too, how long the client has been in business and what its reputation is. Some clients are notoriously hard to collect from. New publications or websites (a.k.a. start-ups) may lack financing. Markets that advertise for writers with promises of exposure or websites that pay per-click aren't good bets. In other cases, you may hear from other sources that the client isn't paying writers.

Finally, make sure you have a written contract *before* you start work on the assignment. An oral agreement may not be enforceable, but an e-mail exchange between you and your editor that sets out the terms—the story topic, word length, payment, rights purchased, and deadline—is better evidence should payment push come to shove.

Writing up your own is simpler than you might imagine. Here's an example:

> DATE
>
> CLIENT'S NAME, TITLE, CONTACT INFO
>
> Dear Mark:
>
> I'm writing to confirm the terms of our agreement as discussed by phone today. Per your assignment, I will write 1,000 words on the benefits of procrastination for MAGAZINE TITLE, for $1,500. The story is due April 1, 2012, and you are purchasing first North American serial rights [the first to publish the piece for the first time in a North American publication] to the piece. Please reply by e-mail to confirm these terms, and thank you for thinking of me. I'm looking forward to working with you.
>
> Sincerely,
> Kelly James-Enger
> [Contact info]

If you don't have a written contract, it's legally presumed that you're selling one-time rights to the story, but that may or may not be your editor's understanding. Without something in writing, you'll have a harder time asserting your rights and collecting payment.

In the event your client still doesn't pay, it's time to play hardball. [See #67, Collect every check.]

63

MAKE EVERY DEADLINE

I am nothing if not reliable. I never missed a deadline as an attorney, and I've never missed one as a freelancer either. And you better believe I use that as a selling point with clients I haven't worked with before.

So, why haven't I missed a deadline? It's not because I'm a compulsive. (I admit that I am.) It's not because I'm a "type-A" personality. (I admit that, too.) It's for one simple reason: I've never taken a deadline I couldn't meet.

Before I accept an assignment, whether it's an article or a book, I estimate how long that story or project will take—not just the *writing* of it, but the research of it as well. A 1,500-word piece that requires several expert interviews, for example, is likely to take less time to research than a shorter article that relies heavily on "real people" sources. I hate real people. Okay, that's not true—I actually love most real people. But I hate having to find and interview them for articles and books. It takes much more time to locate and identify them than it takes to find experts.

I learned this lesson early on. When I accepted an article on the sexual problems newlyweds might face and how to address them, finding experts was a no-brainer. Then I had to find the dreaded "real people"—in this instance, newlyweds who had experienced some kind of sexual challenges and who had sought outside assistance for them. Who would want to *talk* to me about that?! Can you think of anyone? Me neither.

While I had lined up sexual therapists to interview, privacy law prevents them from sharing their patients' names. So I was stuck beating the proverbial bushes for possible sources—and spent weeks making calls, sending e-mails, and begging everyone I could think of to help me with the piece. I did eventually come up with some usable anecdotal sources—thank God my editor let me use pseudonyms—but it still took far longer than I expected. Six weeks, in fact. (My new rule: no more writing about sex.)

Back to deadlines. As I said, I've never missed a deadline because I always make sure I have plenty of time to research, report, and write the piece. Then I build in a bumper. If I think the assignment will take four days, I'll ask for six. If I know I can bang it out in two weeks, I'll try to get two and a half.

Get the idea? I know, considering my current assignments, that I'll be able to meet my deadline before I say yes. Then I start the background research immediately—because after all, I can't interview my sources until I've identified and located those sources. And I can't ask them intelligent questions until I've done my background research. My goal is to get all of my research, including completed interviews, done at least a week before the story is due.

That gives me plenty of time to write and to do any additional research to address questions that crop up as I write the piece—before the deadline is huffing its fetid breath on the back of my neck.

I also use the "double-diary" system to make sure I don't blow a deadline. I write down the assignment in my assignment notebook and then I make a note of it on my calendar. (If you use a program like Outlook, you can do the same thing. Enter it in your program, and make a note of it somewhere else. The idea is that you record every assignment and deadline in two places.)

So, *before* you say yes, make sure you can meet the deadline. If it's going to be tight, ask for more time. And if you know you can't take it on, turn it down and let your client know why. Better to turn down the work than to accept it—and then fail to deliver.

64 FIRE CLIENTS

About five years ago, I had an excellent relationship with a consumer magazine. I did a lot of work for my editor there—features, departments, and even occasional short pieces, which translated to about $25,000/year. The per-word rate wasn't great, but over time, I had asked for more and was making $0.75/word for first North American serial rights and Web rights. I figured it was a fair price, considering that I could resell stories to reprint markets once they ran.

Then my editor left the magazine and the new editor-in-chief instituted an "all-rights" contract across the board, no exceptions. I pleaded my case to her, explaining that I ordinarily don't sell all rights for less than $2/word and that the contract hamstrung me from reselling rights to work in the future. I also pointed out that I'd been a reliable freelancer for the magazine for years, and that I was willing to compromise either on what I was paid or on the terms of the contract.

Still, she wouldn't budge on either aspect. It became a take-it-or-leave-it situation, and I chose to leave it. I completed a story that had been assigned before she came along, and I departed on good terms (I think), but I couldn't justify accepting an all-rights contract for that amount of money. (I admit that today, as the freelance market has changed, my decision might be different.)

As freelancers, we focus on getting clients and maintaining relationships with those clients. But sometimes you'll decide that you no longer want to work with an editor or client.

I've fired clients for the following reasons:

- **TOO MUCH OF A HASSLE.** I'd been working for a custom publisher that only paid $0.50/word. The first couple of pieces went well, but then my editor started insisting on multiple rewrites for the most basic of topics. A story that appeared to be straightforward suddenly took an extra week or two of research, new sources, and sometimes even a new angle by the second go-round. I decided the "hassle factor" was too high and never pitched him again.

- **SLOW PAY.** In another situation, I was writing for a magazine that was having some cash flow problems. It took longer and longer to get paid, and eventually it took me four months (and more than a dozen calls, e-mails, and faxes, culminating in a certified letter threatening legal action) to collect my check for my last piece. And that *was* my last piece for the magazine!

- **TOO LITTLE MONEY.** Early in my freelance career, I did a lot of work for the local newspaper. The stories didn't pay well, but I got a lot of experience interviewing local residents and writing to strict deadlines. After about eighteen months, I realized that the time I was putting into these stories was taking away from time I could be pitching better-paying markets. I needed to move on.
- **CHANGE IN CAREER FOCUS.** I wrote for a trade magazine for years. The work was straightforward, and the money was fair, but when my editor left, I decided not to pitch her replacement. I was devoting more time to writing books, not articles, and continuing my relationship with the publication didn't make sense for my overall career plan.

Of course, there are other reasons to fire a client. Maybe the work is no longer a challenge for you, and you've outgrown the client. Maybe you've determined your hourly rate for the work is too low to justify continuing your relationship. Or maybe you simply dread dealing with the person and have decided life's too short to work with him anymore.

When it comes to how you let a client know he's on your personal "no-fly" list, you have several options. In many instances, I've simply taken the easiest route of no longer pitching the market—and if the market comes to me, I say I'm too busy to take on an assignment. After saying no once or twice, the editor moves on.

In other cases, I've been up-front with the client. With the local newspaper, I explained to my editor there (who'd given me work as an inexperienced newbie!) that I couldn't afford to keep writing stories for her. Not only was she gracious about it, she told me she'd expected it—that a lot of local freelancers followed a similar trajectory, starting with the newspaper and eventually abandoning the work for more lucrative assignments.

In some instances, you may have red flags even before you've started working with the person and decide to cut and run ahead of time. I, too, recently faced a situation where I said no to a new client based on a brief description of his project. The client had an extremely tight deadline in mind (completing his book in five to six weeks) and I didn't think I could make it happen. Plus, I had three separate conferences I was attending/speaking at during that time frame. I realized that I was better off saying no to a lucrative project than losing my mind trying to meet the deadline (and do a good job!), as well as do the other work I already had on my plate.

It's not always easy to fire a client, but one of the benefits of freelancing is that you get to choose who you work for. If you find that the work no longer meets your personal parameters, it's up to you to cut ties so that you have time for the clients who will help you succeed in your career.

USE THE FOUR-PART WORK TEST

When I started freelancing, I said, "Yes, please!" (think *Austin Powers*) to any paying work that came my way. I was trying to make money however I could. My financial goal my first year was to make ... wait for it ... $10,000. I have no idea why I chose that number, other than it was a nice, neat one and seemed realistic for someone launching a freelance business with no connections, no experience, and no clue.

However, having a financial goal (even a small one) made me focus on money, and it meant that every assignment I took that first year had to pay something—even if it was just $25 or $35 for a short piece for the local paper. Even the "small stuff" moved me toward making my income goal that first year. I exceeded my initial goal, grossing more than $17,000 my first year of full-time freelancing.

Today I can't say yes to everything, or even most things. And over time, I've developed a four-part test I use when deciding whether to take on work:

1. **HOW MUCH DOES IT PAY?** (If you're freelancing to make a living, whether full- or part-time, this is obvious.)

2. **HOW LONG WILL IT TAKE?** I've found that the work I've done for national magazines takes far more time (including the pitching and follow-ups) than the work I do for smaller publications. Yes, the big

magazines pay more, but I'm always looking at my hourly rate, not just the size of the check. And sometimes the magazines that pay less per *word* actually pay more per *hour.*

3. **WHAT'S THE PIA FACTOR?** PIA is my shorthand for Pain In the, um, rear end. Some clients and editors are annoying to work with. I'm thinking of an editor I work with who takes forever to respond to queries, then assigns stuff with ridiculously tight deadlines. I love her, but there's definitely a PIA factor to working with her. And if that PIA factor on a particular project is high, I'm either going to get more money ... or I might even walk away.

4. **WILL THIS WORK FURTHER MY CAREER—AND IF SO, HOW?** So, for example, when I wrote my first book, *Ready, Aim, Specialize,* I received an advance of just $2,500. I spent months researching (I interviewed fifty-six sources!) and writing the book. My hourly rate was abysmal. I made more as a teenaged lifeguard.

But here's the thing. I wanted to start writing books, and I had to begin somewhere. So I said yes to the book, added *author* to my CV, and even made royalties from it. My first book led to many others, which has made the first low advance worth it.

As a freelancer, it's within your control to take on work or turn it down. The four-part test has helped me stay on course and prevent me from agreeing to work based only on what it pays. I suggest you look at other factors as well to help you determine what projects meet your short-term and long-term goals.

66 FIGHT FOR YOUR RIGHTS

When I speak at writers conferences, the same questions always come up. How do I find an agent? How can I turn my blog into a book? And should I sign an all-rights contract?

I've seen a definite change in the publishing industry in the last fifteen years. When I started freelancing, I was sometimes offered an all-rights contract. But it was just as likely that an editor sent a more writer-friendly one which asked for "first North American serial rights" (the right to publish the piece in a magazine in North America) and possibly Web, or online, rights as well. Some publications had more than two contracts—the grabby, all-rights one, and the "good" one. If you were smart enough to ask for it, you got the latter.

Publishers are greedier today, and it's not only magazines that want all rights. Many book publishers are asking writers to sign work-for-hire agreements. Technically the only person who can sign a work-for-hire contract is the employee of a company, but the term "work-for-hire" is still used in these agreements. Work-for-hire means that the copyright to the work is held by your employer, or in this case, the publisher. With an all-rights contract, you still hold the copyright to the work, but you transfer all of the rights to your client. There's a legal distinction, but the end result is the same—you've given up all rights to your work, forever.

So do *I* sign all-rights agreements? Short answer is, it depends. Here are the factors to consider before you say yes:

- **HOW MUCH MONEY ARE YOU BEING OFFERED?** The higher the offer, the more likely the chance I'll sign. If it's a low per-word rate, though, I'll probably say no. (For example, *Shape* has an all-rights contract that it won't negotiate on, but I've gotten an editor to pay me $2/word for my work. If I was offered $0.50/word, I'd turn it down.)

- **HOW MUCH TIME WILL THE ASSIGNMENT TAKE?** I've accepted all-rights contracts for simple stories, but I try to retain my rights to longer, more complicated articles because I'm always thinking about what I'm making per-hour, not per-word. However, if I'm offered a lot of money, I still may say yes.

- **HOW LIKELY ARE YOU TO SELL REPRINT RIGHTS TO THE PIECE?** This is a critical question. Some stories have legs; some do not. A short article on an exciting new study or the latest apps for the iPhone has less resale potential than an evergreen topic like helping your kids prepare for the school year or keeping weight off during the holidays. The more likely a piece is to be resold, the more I'll fight to retain reprint rights.

- **WHAT TYPE OF CLIENT IS IT?** Corporations and businesses almost always require you to sign all-rights contracts, as do ghostwriting clients. I expect an all-rights contract in these situations and you should, too. On the other hand, many (but not all) magazine and book publishers are more flexible.
- **HOW ESTABLISHED ARE YOU, CAREER WISE?** As a new freelancer, I signed all-rights contracts without considering the long-term consequences of doing so. I needed clips, checks, and experience. Once I had them, I started trying to negotiate better contracts, often successfully. My point is that inexperienced writers looking for bylines tend to be more willing to sign away their rights than more established writers—and that's understandable.
- **HOW BADLY DO YOU NEED THE WORK?** If you're writing for a living, and your workload is light, you may have to take on a contract you'd normally bypass. It may also be a topic you desperately want to write about but have been unable to sell elsewhere. Only you can determine how much the assignment is worth to you.

Rather than signing an all-rights contract as is, or choosing to walk away from the offer, don't forget that you have another option—to change the contract language. If a publisher is concerned about exclusivity, for example, you can offer not to resell the story for a specific period of time. For example, instead of selling all rights to a story, I was able to get the editor to purchase exclusive North American serial rights for six months; after that, I was free to resell the piece. We used the same contract language for the next dozen stories I wrote for her, too.

As a freelancer, it's up to you to decide whether to agree to an all-rights contract, and I certainly understand why you would, and why I have in the past, and no doubt will again. Just consider what you're getting—and what you're giving up—before you sign.

67

COLLECT EVERY CHECK

As a freelancer, you make money by selling your words. But what happens when you perform the work, yet a client fails to pay you for it?

This will happen to you at some point in your freelance career, but there are steps you can take to get paid almost every time. Always have a written contract [see #62, Plan on payment], send an invoice when necessary, and follow up on outstanding invoices promptly, and you'll collect on your accounts receivable.

After you've signed a contract and completed your assignment, ask your client whether she needs an invoice to pay you. In many cases, an editor will simply "put payment through," and you'll receive a check. If you need to supply an invoice, though, you can use software like QuickBooks or write one yourself. Include your client's name, the project, what rights you're selling (or you can say "according to written contract dated January 1, 2012"), the amount of money, your social security number or tax ID number, and your contact information. I always include an invoice number for easier tracking.

Here's an example:

> DATE
>
> EDITOR'S NAME/CONTACT INFO
>
> Re: INVOICE #387
>
> Dear Sue,
> Please let this letter serve as my invoice for $90 for one-time reprint rights to "Banish the Workout Blues" per your e-mail of today. My Social Security number is xxx-xx-xxxx.
>
> Thank you very much!
> Best,
> Kelly James-Enger
> [mailing address]

Good enough. But what if you don't get paid right away? Then it's time for a follow-up letter like the following:

DATE

EDITOR'S NAME/CONTACT INFO

Re: INVOICE #387

Dear Sue,

I'm reviewing my accounts receivable and realize I haven't yet been paid for the above-referenced invoice, for $90 for one-time reprint rights to "Banish the Workout Blues." Could you please let me know when I can expect payment?

Thank you very much for your time and help.

Best,
Kelly James-Enger
[mailing address]

And if you still don't get paid, then it's time for what I call the "pay-or-die" letter. You'll want to detail the terms of your contract, prove that you've satisfied your contractual obligations, and describe the attempts you've taken to get paid. I've found that threatening legal action usually provokes payment.

One more thing—find out who actually cuts the checks (it's not your editor) and pursue her directly. That will get you paid quicker.

Here's an example of a letter I sent to the owner of a publishing company that had owed me money for months, with names changed to protect the guilty:

DATE

Dear Mr. Badman:
I am a full-time freelance writer who has spent over six months trying to collect payment for work performed for *No-pay* magazine. I first sent invoices for the work last August after my articles were accepted but have never been paid for them.

In the past two months alone, I have sent two letters with copies of invoices to Michael Nogood, your controller, and have called him on nine occasions. He has never returned my calls nor paid me for the outstanding sums owed me. Your company still owes me the following amounts:

Story/Issue/Amount

"Fit on the Street"/November/December, 1999/$270.45

"Ten Health Club Commandments"/January/February, 2000/$750.00

TOTAL $1,020.45

As all of this work was long since performed (back in the summer of 1999) and these issues have already been published, I would appreciate it if you would immediately issue me a check for $1,020.45. If I don't receive payment within five days, I'll turn the matter over for collection and will involve my attorney.

Thank you for your prompt attention to this matter. I look forward to hearing from you and receiving my check soon.

Very truly yours,
Kelly James-Enger

With this letter, I did get paid, finally. (And no, I didn't write for this publication again.)

Getting a written contract for any work you do is the first step to collecting every check you're owed. Keeping accurate written records and following up on outstanding invoices (even if you must do it multiple times) will help you turn your accounts receivables into actual money.

QUESTION RESEARCH CLAIMS

As a freelancer, you're expected to research the topics you're writing about. If you write about any aspect of health and wellness, you'll need to know how to find research studies and interpret them. (Even if you don't specialize in health, the ability to decode research studies is a valuable skill for any freelancer to have.)

To locate any health-related study (including fitness, nutrition, and psychology), check out PubMed www.ncbi.nlm.nih.gov/pubmed, the search engine of the U.S. National Library of Medicine. Finding a study on the subject is the first step; second, read the abstract, a paragraph that gives a brief explanation of the study and its findings, to determine whether you want to read the entire study.

The full text of some articles is available online for no charge. Most other studies can be ordered through online databases for a fee, but to save money, check with your local library to see if it can obtain it for you. Your library may have access to databases you do not and can otherwise order research studies for patrons. Typically there's a small charge involved (for example, my library charges three dollars if it has to search out-of-state sources) and it takes about a week to get a hard copy or PDF of the study.

But you need the full text of any study you reference in an article for "backup" or fact-checking. More important, you need to read the entire study to understand its significance.

In general, the larger the study, the better. In other words, a study conducted on 50,00 people holds more weight than one conducted on several hundred. And I say people for a reason—hundreds of thousands of published articles are on animals, not people—and those kinds of results aren't always duplicated in humans. It's okay to cite an animal study if that's all you have, but your article should make it clear that the subjects were, say, mice, not people.

Reading the study will tell you whether it is an observational study (for example, the Nurses' Health Study), where subjects were observed and tracked over time. Or it might be an interventional study, where subjects had their lifestyle changed in some way (such as by being given a particular medication or changing their diet) and then were compared to people (called the control group) who didn't make those changes. (If there's no control group, it's more difficult to measure the impact of the intervention.) A review article, on the other hand, simply reviews the research on a particular subject.

When reading a research study, keep these questions in mind:

- Was the study randomized and double-blind (meaning that the researchers themselves were unaware of which subjects comprised the control group and which were the experimental)? Was it a controlled study, meaning that the researchers sought to change only one variable and keep other possible variables consistent?

- What were the demographics of the people involved? Were both men and women included? What ages were they? How were they selected to participate in the study? Was the sample of subjects truly random, or not? For example, in a survey, people are often self-selected—meaning that they opted to participate. Another issue is that when people are surveyed for results (as having the results tracked by the researchers) they often underreport "negative" and overreport "positive" behavior. So, when surveyed, people almost always underestimate the amount of calories they consume, for example, and overestimate how active they are.

- Was it an animal or human study? The results of an animal study can *suggest* what may happen in humans but is never considered conclusive. To know how something will affect people, well, you have to try it out on people.

- Was the study conducted by a major university or hospital? Was it a truly independent study or was it underwritten in whole or in part by a corporation or association that may have a vested interest in the results of the research (for example, a bottled-water supplier supporting a study on how much water is needed for optimal health)?

- Did the results confirm or agree with existing research or were the results surprising? Why? What makes it different or similar to other research in the field? Is it a truly a groundbreaking study of something that basically repeats earlier research?

Here's an example. A study published in 2005 found that overweight participants who ate an egg-based breakfast compared to a bagel-based breakfast (both breakfasts contained the same number of calories) ate 164 fewer calories for lunch than those who had the bagel breakfasts. So, the takeaway message is that eating eggs boosts satiety and can help promote weight loss—and that makes a great cover line.

But a closer look at the study itself reveals that only thirty people participated in the study, and they ate each breakfast only once. Second, the participants were all overweight women. (Maybe men wouldn't have experienced the same level of satiety? Maybe normal-weight women would have eaten the same amount regardless of the type of breakfast? Who knows?). But third, and most important, if you look at the footnotes of the study, you'll see that the funding was from the Egg Nutrition Center, United States Department of Agriculture. And part of the mission of the ENC is to "promote eggs as a nutritious, convenient, safe, and affordable contributor to the balance and variety of a nutritious diet." Would I still include this study in an article? Yes, but I would also disclose the ENC's funding.

As a freelancer, your job is to do some digging to determine how legitimate the study actually is. Same goes for when a source gives you a quote or statistic—ask what they're basing their information on. That kind of legwork will make you a better reporter and make you more valuable to your editors, regardless of what subjects you cover.

69 FORGET ROYALTIES

Would-be book authors usually don't understand the way advances and royalties work. Since I started ghostwriting, I've had dozens of people contact me with great ideas for guaranteed bestsellers. They're never willing to pay me up-front, but I'm assured of making hundreds of thousands (if not millions) on royalties. I spend a lot of time educating these people about how the publishing world works—and explaining why I won't write any book based on the royalties.

As a freelancer, you should understand how advances and royalties work. When a traditional publisher acquires the rights to a book, it usually pays an advance, which is technically an "advance against royalties." A royalty is the percentage you're paid for each book sale as its author. If and when that advance is made back (which is called "earning out"), you begin to earn royalties. If a book doesn't earn enough to pay back the advance, you'll never see royalties.

Understand that earning out and a publisher's break-even number are not the same. The publisher is going to spend a certain amount of money for the advance, production, marketing, and distribution of the book. When that amount of money is made back (and you'll never know what that magic number is), the publisher starts making a profit. You don't make royalties, though, until your book has earned out.

So, what kind of advance will you get? It depends on your book, the publisher, and your all-important platform. I've written books that received advances as low as $2,500 and as high as $55,000.

Unfortunately, average advances are shrinking. This is in part due to the economy (publishing's a business like any other) and in part due to the glut of celebrity books hitting the shelves. When Snooki and The Situation (both of *Jersey Shore* "fame") get book deals, that's bad news for midlist authors like me. The more money publishers shell out for these kinds of titles, the less they have to spend on noncelebrity authors like myself.

You can forget the idea of getting rich on royalties. Four out of five books don't earn out, which means that the advance is all the money you're likely to see for your book. That's why I assume that the advance I receive for a book is the only money I'll make on it. I love being pleasantly surprised (about half of my books pay royalties), but I don't count on that money.

Let me give an example so you can understand how this works. When I sold *Six-Figure Freelancing* to Random House in 2003, I received an advance of $15,000. *Six-Figure Freelancing* was published in 2005 with a cover price of $14.95. The escalation clause in my contract means that my royalty works out to be $.89/book for the first 10,000 sold, $1.12/book for every book thereafter. (I make considerably more, $3.88/book, for every electronic version that sells.)

Every six months I receive a royalty statement from Random House that tells me how many copies I sold in a specific six-month period, and how quickly (or slowly) I'm approaching my "earned out" figure. *Six-Figure Freelancing* sold about 4,600 copies in 2005, the first year it was published, and about 1,200 copies annually since then.

My most recent royalty statement for this book covers the six-month period ending September 30, 2010. During that time, I sold 82 e-books (a total of $318.49), and 338 trade paperbacks (for a total of $372.29). Total copies sold during this period was 420. This is the lowest amount of sales I've ever had in a six-month period, but the highest number of e-book sales. (For comparison, during the previous six months, I had sold 40 e-books and 478 trade paperbacks, for a total of 519 copies.)

More important, so far, my cumulative sales equals 142 e-books and 11,378 trade paperbacks, a total of 11,520 copies. That's not bad. My total royalties are $10,939.83, which includes $273.68 of subsidiary rights income from licensing rights to a book club.

However, the most important figure to my mind is $4,060.17, or the difference between my earned royalties and my advance. Once the book produces that amount of royalties, I'll start earning additional royalties, but until that happens, it's Random House that's making money on the book right now, not me.

Bottom line? If you write books, push for the biggest advance you can get. There's a good chance that's all the money you'll see from that book.

COMPREHEND COPYRIGHT

As a freelancer, you make a living from your words. That's why I'm always so surprised at how few writers actually understand what copyright is—and how to protect it.

Here's the least every freelancer needs to know about copyright:

1. When you write an article, book proposal, or book on your own, you automatically own the copyright to it.
2. You retain copyright, or ownership, of the work unless and until you sell, transfer, or grant the copyright to someone else.

That's it! But let's talk about what copyright actually is. According to the U.S. Copyright Office, copyright is a form of protection provided by U.S. law to the authors of "original works of authorship," including literary, dramatic, musical, artistic, and certain other intellectual rights. Copyright means that the author of the work has the exclusive right to do what he wishes with his work and to authorize others to do the same.

So, as the copyright owner, you (and only you) can do whatever you want with the work you've created—until and unless you sell, transfer, or assign those rights to someone else, like a publisher. That's copyright law in a nutshell.

New writers often think they have to register their work with the Library of Congress to create copyright. That's not true. Copyright protection is created concurrently with the work—as you get the words down on the page (what the law refers to as "in fixed form"), it's automatically copyrighted. But it has to be "in fixed form." An idea is not in fixed form and so isn't protected by copyright law.

Of course, there is an exception to every rule. With copyright, the exception is when you are an employee, creating work for an employer. Then the company you work for owns the copyright to anything you create at work under what's called the work-for-hire doctrine. In that case, your employer, not you, automatically owns the writing you do at work. (Some freelance contracts also have work-for-hire provisions; legally speaking, though, a work-for-hire can only exist between an employer and an employee, not a freelancer and a client.)

COPYRIGHT NOTICE

Simple enough. So then, what's with the copyright symbol (©)? Why do people stick that on written work? The reason has to do with something called the "innocent infringement" doctrine.

Copyright notice simply lets everyday people (i.e., those who know nothing about publishing law) that this work is someone's property. If there's no copyright notice on a piece of writing and someone copies or uses it for their own purposes (assuming in good faith that it's okay to do so—what the courts call an "innocent infringer"), that person may not be liable for damages. That's why notice is required—to let would-be innocent infringers know that they can't use your work.

The notice required is the copyright symbol ©, followed by the date the work was first published, and the author's name—for example, © 2012, Kelly James-Enger. That's why books have a copyright page—to help protect the work from no-longer-innocent infringers. Just keep in mind that if you're sending work out to anyone in the publishing biz—agents, editors, or publishers—you needn't stick a copyright notice on your work. *They* know it's copyrighted—and it looks amateurish.

WHY REGISTER YOUR WORK?

There's one last thing about copyright that freelancers should keep in mind. Yes, your work is automatically protected by copyright simply by writing it. But if you want *effective* protection, you should register it with the Library of Congress. To pursue a copyright infringement case, it's easier and more lucrative if you have registered your work "in a timely fashion" (within three months of publication) with the LOC.

The copyright statute provides that if you prevail, you can get attorneys' fees (which can easily reach tens of thousands of dollars) and statutory damages—in other words, monetary damages set out by law. (Contrast this to having to *prove* your damages in court, which is much more difficult.) If you've registered your copyright, you can introduce that fact at trial to prove you're the legal copyright owner. That's big. Now, if you don't register your work within three months after it's published, you may still have a cause of action for infringement, but you're limited to injunctive relief and/or actual damages—that is, the amount of money you have lost because of the violator's actions, which may be impossible to conclusively prove.

So, once your work is published, you have three months to register it. (Registering is retroactive, which means that registering within those three months protects you back to the publication date.) At the time of writing, fees to register with the U.S. Copyright Office were:

- $35 to register work online;
- $50 to register work via paper registration; and
- $65 to register a group of articles or other work for periodicals or database updates.

For more information about copyright registration procedures, visit www.copyright.gov. You'll find the forms you need at www.copyright.gov/forms.

The bottom line? Any co-authoring or ghostwriting contract should set out who owns the copyright to the work you're creating. And make sure that your client understands the importance of actually registering his copyright, unless he's working with a traditional publisher that will do it for him. A registered copyright is the best weapon to protect your work.

KNOW YOUR DAILY NUT

You already know that I think freelancers should focus more on dollars/hour, not dollars/word. But there's another figure you should always have in mind—what I call your daily nut.

The daily nut is the amount you have to average to meet your annual income goal.

Say your annual income goal is $60,000. (According to a survey I conducted in 2011, 28 percent of freelancers are making $60,000 or more annually.) While there's 365 days in a year (366 in a leap year), let's assume you're not going to work seven days a week—I know I don't! So let's plan on working five days a week, fifty weeks a year, with two weeks off for vacation.

Grossing $60,000 a year over 250 workdays comes to $240 a day. That number, $240, is your daily nut. Instead of thinking about making $60,000, which can seem unreachable, focus on meeting your daily goal—and then track your progress.

If you're new to freelancing, your daily nut may be lower. My goal for my second year of full-time freelancing, for example, was to make $36,000.

As I was working forty-eight weeks out of the year (taking four weeks off for vacation and holidays), that meant I had to make $150/day. And when I aimed to break the six-figure barrier my sixth year of full-time freelancing, my daily nut was $400.

The daily nut keeps you focused on how you're working. Every day, you should average this amount of income, or you won't hit your financial goal at year's end. If your daily nut is $250, an article that pays $1,000 should take you about four days' worth of work. A book proposal that pays $4,500 should take about eighteen days' worth of work, total. Of course, not every project will work out exactly like this—some will take more time, some will take less. The idea, though, is that you average a certain amount each day.

Regardless of how long you've been freelancing, if you're writing to make money, I suggest you calculate, and track, your daily nut. It will help you treat your writing like a business—which it is.

SET BOTH KINDS OF GOALS

Setting goals forces you to take a closer look at your writing priorities and get a handle on what's really important to you. Writers who have heard me speak know that I divide goals into two types—overall, or "outcome" goals and production, or "performance" goals. Overall goals tend to be biggies—you know, like writing a novel, finding a publisher for your nonfiction book project, or finally ditching your day job to freelance full-time.

The problem with outcome goals is that they don't help you actually achieve your aim. That's where performance, or production, goals come in. They're the actionable goals that move you toward your outcome goal. To be effective, they should be SMART, or Specific, Measurable, Attainable, Realistic, and Time-based.

For example, my income goal for the coming year is to make $60,000. That's my *outcome* goal. My performance goal is to make $250/day for 240 days/year, working an average of fifteen hours/week. (This figure also fits with the average rate of $100/hour I try to maintain, and it is realistic considering what I made in 2010 and the types of work I do.) Get it?

Think both big (your long-term aims) and small (e.g., meeting your daily nut) when you're setting goals. After you've decided what they are, write them down, and track your progress in the coming weeks.

Let's say you've been writing for regional magazines and want to break into nationals. That's your outcome goal with only two possible outcomes—you'll either make it or you won't. While you can strive to achieve it, in the end, whether you will make it may depend, at least in part, on luck, timing, or an editor's hurried last-minute decision.

So you need to set some performance, or production, goals as well. Yours might include researching a certain number of new markets each month, querying a certain number of editors each week, and sending follow-up letters to editors who haven't responded in a certain period of time. Each of these is specific, measurable, attainable, realistic, and time-based.

Production goals aren't sexy, but they enable you to focus on specific things you *can* do to further your writing career. They also break up a seemingly insurmountable goal into a series of small, manageable steps. You want to write a novel by the end of the year? Then your production goal might be to write one page a day, produce five pages every week, or to write for thirty minutes every evening before going to bed.

Regardless of what path you're on, your goals should reflect your overall objectives as a freelancer. Don't be afraid to tweak them throughout the year as your circumstances change. SMART goals give you a road map to follow, but you can always choose to take a different route to your destination.

KNOW WHAT YOU CAN DEDUCT

I don't know any freelancer who enjoys talking about taxes, let alone paying them. But a basic understanding of what you must pay to Uncle Sam—and what you can legitimately deduct—is essential to your success.

Let's take a quick jaunt through the relevant tax law. First, when you're self-employed, *all* money you receive from clients (even if it's to reimburse you for expenses) must be reported as income to the Internal Revenue Service. (Actually this is true for any kind of income you take in, even if it's from holding a garage sale. You're expected to report and pay taxes on every dollar you make.)

However, if you're in the writing *business*, as opposed to writing as a hobbyist (the category that most writers fall into), then you can deduct legitimate business expenses from the total amount of money you make (your gross income) and only pay taxes on the difference, which is called your net.

The IRS takes a number of factors into account to determine whether you treat your writing as actual business or if it's more of a hobby for you. The primary factor is the presence of a "profit motive." In other words, you're freelancing to make money.

When you're a self-employed writer, not a hobbyist, you can deduct all ordinary, necessary, and reasonable expenses that are incurred as you run your business and try (and hopefully succeed) to make it a profit from it. For freelancers, those expenses typically include:

- Computer (doesn't matter if you're a PC or a Mac!) and other office peripherals like a scanner/copier;
- Office supplies like paper, printer cartridges, business cards, pens, highlighters, and thank-you notes;
- Postage/mailing costs;
- Membership fees to professional organizations for freelancers;
- Office equipment—e.g., desk, office chair, and file cabinets;
- Travel and entertainment related to your business (for example, flying to interview key sources or taking a client out to lunch. However, while you can deduct all of your work-related travel expenses, you can only take 50 percent of work-related meals/entertainment);
- Internet access, website hosting, and other online fees;

- Telephone expenses (you can't deduct the expense of your primary phone line, but you can deduct long-distance charges related to your business, as well as the cost of a second phone line and/or cell phone solely used for business); and
- Car expenses. The majority of self-employed writers use the standard mileage deduction, which in 2011 was $0.51/mile for the first six months of the year and $0.55/mile for the second half of the year. If you prefer, the IRS allows you to use a more complicated formula that's based on the amount you use your vehicle for business and personal use.

In addition, if you're self-employed, you may be able to deduct the cost of medical insurance premiums for yourself, your spouse, and your family. You may also be able to take a home office deduction if you work from home and use a section of it (be it a room or part of a room) *solely and exclusively* as your place of business. (Don't worry—you can still work at your local coffee shop for a change of scene. I'm a regular at my favorite Caribou Coffee. But *most* of your work should be done from your home office, and you shouldn't be doing anything that's not work related there either.)

I'm not a tax professional (hey, I'm not even a lawyer anymore), so if you have questions, talk to an accountant or visit www.IRS.gov for more info. (The *Tax Guide for Small Business*, Publication 334, is especially helpful.) Track all of your writing-related expenses and keep your receipts so in the rare event you're audited, you have proof of what you spent on your business, when, and why.

CONSIDER OPPORTUNITY COST

I use the four-part work test when I decide whether to take on an assignment. I consider how much money I'll make and how much time the work will take, along with two other factors before I say yes to work. [See #65, Use the four-part work test.]

But there's another factor to consider that most freelancers overlook. It's what businesspeople call opportunity cost.

Opportunity cost is the work you're unable to perform because you've taken on that particular assignment. Typically the bigger or more complex the assignment, the greater its opportunity cost. And the tighter the deadline is, the higher the opportunity cost is likely to be, because you'll be busting your butt to make that deadline, which means you have less time for other projects.

For example, at the end of last year, I signed two new ghostwriting clients, both with aggressive deadlines. That was awesome news for my business and my bank account, but it also meant that I couldn't take on any other major projects (even lucrative ones) in the meantime. I knew how much work I could handle (and I have two kiddos to wrangle as well), and between that and the holidays, I was already overbooked.

But even smaller assignments can carry a sizeable opportunity cost as well. When I started freelancing, I wrote articles for my local newspaper. The pieces averaged about $50 and usually required a trip out of the office to attend an event or interview a source in person. It wasn't long before I realized that I needed to eliminate the paper as a client.

It wasn't a difficult decision. First, the pay wasn't much, yet the stories usually took several hours to research because I did in-person interviews before I went home to write them up. The real problem, though, was that the time I spent researching and writing the stories prevented me from pitching more lucrative markets (like national magazines) that would result in better-paying work. That's opportunity cost, and it was hurting me both in the short- and long-term.

So, *before* you take on an assignment, especially one that has a tight deadline or requires a lot of time, consider its opportunity cost. I also suggest that at the end of every year, as you're evaluating what kinds of work you did and where your income came from, you consider the opportunity cost of your regular clients.

Is the amount of money they pay you worth the hassles, time, or potential loss of other, more lucrative work? Only you can determine what the opportunity cost of a particular assignment or client is, and whether that assignment or client is worth it. Just remember that when you say yes to one project, you may be saying no to another.

DIVERSIFY YOUR WORK

When I started freelancing, I planned to write magazine articles and work on my novel. That was my business plan.

I learned pretty quickly, though, that magazine articles weren't enough. I was pitching dozens of different magazines, but my query success rate wasn't very high. Even if I did get an assignment, months elapsed between the time I first pitched an idea, its eventual assignment, and getting paid for it. That meant my cash flow looked more like a dribble. I broke free from my original plan and diversified. I started "stringing," or freelancing, for my local paper and writing for a variety of local businesses, which paid much more quickly. By the end of the year, my cash flow and workload were much more consistent. [See #79, Beat the feast-or-famine syndrome.]

Diversifying isn't just practical; it's smart. Your ability to perform a variety of different kinds of work makes you more marketable to clients and ensures that you keep up with an ever-changing freelance market. [See #80, Boost your value.]

My 2011 survey of more than two hundred full-time freelancers revealed that they're performing a wide array of work which includes:

- Blogging (whether they blog for others or produce income from their own blogs)
- Editing (all types)
- Ghostwriting (books, articles, blogs)
- Proofreading
- Public speaking

- SEO (search engine optimization) writing
- Teaching (in-person and online)
- Writing articles for academic magazines
- Writing articles for consumer magazines
- Writing articles for custom magazines
- Writing articles for newspapers
- Writing articles for online markets
- Writing articles for trade magazines
- Writing books (whether traditionally published, POD, or e-books)
- Writing for corporations/businesses
- Writing for nonprofit organizations

That's sixteen different types of work, and it only scratches the surface of what freelancers are doing today. Don't get stuck doing just one or two kinds of writing; the more versatile you are, the more clients you'll be able to attract and the better you'll weather changes in the publishing world.

76 PLAN TO PROMOTE

Last year I spoke at the Annual Writer's Institute in Madison, Wisconsin. My most popular session was on book publishing options and the pros and cons of each. Today authors have a choice between traditional publishing, print-on-demand (POD) publishing, true self-publishing (where you become your own publisher), and e-books. The majority of titles fall into the first two categories, although e-books are the fastest growing subcategory.

When it came time for questions, a woman raised her hand. "I understand what you're saying about how important it is to sell your book," she said. "I have a blog and I'm on social media and I'm promoting the hell out of my book. But I just want a traditional publisher to pick it up so I don't have to do that anymore!"

I said, "I don't want to put you on the spot, but did you hear what you just said? You said you don't want to sell your book anymore. But even if a traditional publisher does pick it up, you're *still* going to have to sell it. That's the whole idea. No matter *how* your book is published, your job as the author is to sell it."

I could tell she was disappointed, but that's the truth. Believe me, I get it. I don't want to *sell* books either! I want to write them! Most authors become authors because they love to write, not because they love to market and promote. But if you're not willing to promote and sell your books, you'll fail as a book author, at least if your goals include selling lots of books and/or making money from your books, which I hope they do.

There's no shortage of books and websites that tell you how to promote your book, and many POD companies now offer marketing services to authors as well. The bottom line, though, is what works for one book won't work for another. Your understanding of your readership—who they are and how you can connect with them—is the key to deciding how you'll spend your marketing time and dollars.

For example, my book on ghostwriting, *Goodbye Byline, Hello Big Bucks*, is aimed at a fairly narrow audience: freelancers and authors who want to add ghostwriting to their repertoire, or want to learn more about this field. Those are the people I want to promote my book to, so here are some of the ways I tried to reach them:

- I launched my blog, Dollars and Deadlines, when I started writing the book, to create a built-in readership and hopefully buyers once the book was published.
- I added an "Author" page on Facebook, signed up for Twitter, and started following people. (Yes, this was in 2010. I admit to being behind on my social media strategy.)

- I asked for, and received, a cover blurb from Marcia Layton Turner, founder and executive director of the Association of Ghostwriters.
- I pitched articles on ghostwriting to a variety of writer's publications and wrote a six-page feature on ghostwriting that ran in the April 2011 issue of *Writer's Digest*.
- I wrote guest posts for a variety of writing-related blogs and participated in teleseminars with sites like The Renegade Writer.
- I requested that *The ASJA Monthly* review my book (and it received a glowing recommendation).
- I e-mailed editors, former clients, former students, and other writers, telling them about the book.
- I arranged to speak at writers conferences, where I presented on ghostwriting and/or sold my book.
- I brought copies of my book to all of my speaking gigs so attendees could buy copies if they wanted.
- I asked readers who got in touch with me after buying the book to post reviews on Amazon.com, and to recommend the book to friends.

Here's the thing: This may sound like a lot, but it's pretty minimal, and the work is only beginning. I published this book via POD, which means I have no publisher doing anything, so it's up to me to sell the book.

Regardless of which publishing option you choose, I suggest that you devote several months of full-time work promoting your book when it's first published. Then plan to continue to promote it however you can for the next couple of years. If you can't commit to that, you may want to question whether becoming an author is a smart career move.

BLOG WITH PURPOSE

Seems like everyone I know has a blog. No problem. But if you're a freelancer, I suggest you blog with a purpose—either to make money, to sell books, to build your platform, or to attract clients. In other words, you blog not just for pleasure but also for bucks.

Freelancer Jane Boursaw was blogging, and making money for it, long before most of us had even considered trying to master the form. Boursaw, who writes about entertainment, started her blog to accompany her main website, ReelLifeWithJane.com. Today, "it still serves as a 'moving picture show' to my main website, www.reellifewithjane.com, which holds clips, testimonials, syndication info for editors, a list of syndication partners, links to my social media networks, full-length movie reviews, and other related info," says Boursaw.

"My blog has actually become an income earner in its own right, as blogging there consistently has attracted the interest of advertisers and sponsors," says Boursaw. "The blog, along with my syndicated family movie and TV reviews, online blogging classes and one-on-one mentoring (www.writebloglearn.com), makes up the bulk of my income, all of which supports my family of four."

Sounds great, huh? But it's not as simple as just deciding to blog and then watching the cash roll in. "I always tell my blogging students to choose a topic that you're truly passionate about, because it's something you'll live with every day," cautions Boursaw. You needn't plan on blogging *every* day, but you should plan on posting at least once or twice a week, preferably the same days so your readers want to visit regularly.

Do plenty of planning, including identifying the reasons for your blog and identifying your audience, *before* you launch yours. I played with the idea of blogging for several years (and took Boursaw's excellent blogging e-class), considering and discarding potential topics before I settled on one that stuck. My blog, *Dollars and Deadlines*, was created for four primary reasons:

- To sell copies of my new book on ghostwriting, *Goodbye Byline, Hello Big Bucks*, once it was published;
- To continue to sell copies of my older freelance-related books;
- To attract potential ghostwriting and collaborating clients; and
- To continue to build my platform as a freelancing expert.

My blog's tagline is "Helping nonfiction freelancers make more money in less time." That identifies both the purpose and audience of my blog. While I occasionally stray from the strictest interpretation of this phrase, my blog posts always relate to the challenges and benefits of freelancing. My readers know what to expect every time they visit.

So, make sure you've identified your audience and your purpose before you jump in. There's nothing wrong with blogging because you'd like to write and sell a book. It's becoming a common way to nab a publishing deal, especially when your platform is still in progress. [See #13, Create a platform.] My friend Polly Campbell started her blog, www.imperfectspirituality.com, to help build a readership and sell her book of the same name, and a traditional publisher picked it up. Freelancer Denise Schipani's blog, www.confessionsofameanmommy.com, got her noticed and led to her first book deal, too, for *Mean Mom, Good Mom*.

If you're ready to blog for bucks, Boursaw offers these five successful blogging keys:

1. Pick a topic you love.
2. Create a business where your blog blends well or is the foundation for the rest of your business.
3. Have faith in your abilities and your message, whatever that may be.
4. Always, always, always provide quality content on your blog, whether the post is short or long. Great writing is what sets the professional blogs apart from the rest of the pack.
5. Network with other bloggers and people in your niche as much as possible. Spend time on Twitter and Facebook and join groups with like-minded bloggers. If there isn't a group for your niche, start one.

Boursaw's blog supports and builds her syndication business, and vice versa. It's her version of double-dipping. "The blog is also a great foundation for my syndicated family movie and TV reviews, because it gives my syndication partners added value when they sign on with me," she explains. She writes weekly "Family Publication Spotlights" on her blog to highlight individual magazines and websites that run her reviews, and allows her syndication partners to swipe any of her blog content, including images, as long as they provide a byline and a link back to her site.

Boursaw has found that the more she blogs, the more readers she draws, and the more advertisers and syndicators she gets. While you may not have as much success with yours, I suggest you blog for more than pleasure. Your blog should, at the minimum, attract new clients and build your platform. Hopefully it will do much more.

GET IN FRONT OF THE ROOM

I'm a big fan of double-dipping, my term for doing more than one kind of paying work at a time. When I reslant an idea, I'm double-dipping. When I sell reprints, I'm double-dipping. When I write articles and books about the same subject, I'm double-dipping.

And when I speak *and* sell books, I'm double-dipping. That's because as a professional speaker, I get paid to present and I often can sell books as well (what speakers call back-of-the-room sales). But as a speaker and an author, I've had to decide which takes first priority. If you do both—write books and speak as well—you must do the same. In other words, are you an author who wants to sell her book, or are you a speaker who happens to be an author as well?

Here's the thing: As the former (an author with a book to sell), people will expect you to speak for free. After all, you want to sell your book, so you're probably willing to show up anywhere and everywhere (think bookstores, book clubs, luncheons, and conferences) to promote your book, which will hopefully result in book sales and eventual royalties. And that's fine—that's what I did with my first couple of titles. I put a lot of miles on my car and took a lot of time away from my business to sell as many books as possible.

But along the way, I began to speak professionally, focusing on topics including healthy lifestyles. I had started out doing writing programs at writers conferences and local libraries, but as a health and fitness writer, I soon branched out to covering health and lifestyle subjects for corporations and associations. These gigs paid much better even if I didn't sell any books, and I made a conscious choice: to give up speaking solely to sell books. Speaking for free (even if I sell a few books) is simply not worth my time. And it devalues my work as a speaker.

If you're a speaker who happens to have a book to sell, you don't speak for free, or just for exposure for your title. You speak to make money and hope to make extra income with back-of-the-room sales. That means you get paid twice—once for the speaking gig and once for any books you sell while there. That's the double-dip technique I use.

So, how do you get paid to speak? First, develop your speaking skills. I'd been a lawyer, so I was comfortable in front of an audience, but I spent several years attending conferences and watching (and listening) to dozens of speakers to see which techniques worked. If you get the sweats at the idea of speaking in front of a group, join a local Toastmasters chapter or check out the National Speakers Association for programs that can help you improve.

Choose a topic or area to cover as a speaker. Don't offer to speak about anything and everything—consider what you've written about to develop a list of speaking topics. I started out by teaching magazine writing at my local community college and then contacted area libraries to see if they were interested in having me present writing-related programs. After I coauthored a book on health and fitness (*Small Changes, Big Results*), I used that to expand my program list to related topics. Today, in addition to speaking about writing-related subjects, I offer programs on healthy habits, stress management, and time management.

Starting out, contact libraries, bookstores, book clubs, and service groups like the Lions to see if they'd be interested in having you present. You won't be paid, but the idea is to gain experience and confidence—and then you can start charging, say $150–200/appearance. I charge $300 for library presentations and significantly more than that for corporate and other gigs.

Speaking, like writing, is a skill. One that you can always improve. Here are five ways to give a killer presentation, even when you're new to doing so:

- *Practice ahead of time.* Time yourself so you know how long your presentation will take. Your speech should include three to five major points; structure it so it has a clear beginning, middle and end. If you haven't prepared, your audience will know, believe me.
- *Use notes.* Write an outline, and print it out in large font to stay on track. But don't read your speech word for word, or read your PowerPoint slides line by line (there's nothing more boring!). Look out at your audience and make eye contact with listeners to connect with them and maintain their attention.
- *Focus on your open and close.* Always start a speech with an attention getter (like a relatable story) and close with an uplifting, motivating call to action. According to the primacy and recency effect, your listeners will remember the first thing you say and the last thing you say. Yes, your middle should be good, too, but the open and close should be stellar.
- *Use anecdotes.* Listeners are more likely to remember a story than a rule or lesson. Include war stories to illustrate your major points.
- *Be funny.* I don't tell jokes when I speak, but I do strive to be entertaining. Make your audience laugh, and they'll like you. Make them laugh more than once, and they'll be more likely to remember what you say. (Laughter increases the blood supply to the brain, enhancing memory.)

Speaking isn't for every writer, but if you plan on becoming a book author, you need to be good at it. Add it to your freelancing repertoire and speaking can help you develop your platform, attract new clients, and sell books. Get good enough at it and you can charge for it, too, adding to your overall freelance income.

79

BEAT THE FEAST-OR-FAMINE SYNDROME

No matter how experienced they are, all freelancers (including me) struggle with an ongoing issue. It's what I call the feast-or-famine syndrome. In other words, you're either swamped with work to the point that you're chained to the PC—or you have so little to do that you're overcome with simultaneous boredom, malaise, and hand-wringing anxiety.

Which is worse? The slow times, for sure. Every freelancer I know would rather be insanely busy than bored and broke. Wouldn't you?

But when you're busy, it's all too easy to forget about marketing—that is, until you crawl out from under a bunch of assignments and discover you have no work waiting for you. That's why I try to ensure a steady stream of work by mentally dividing assignments into three categories: **category A**, work that's been completed, turned in, and accepted (and that I'm awaiting payment on); **category B**, work that's been turned in but is awaiting approval by the editor or client; and **category C**, work that's "on my desk" that's been assigned but still has to be researched and written.

Maintaining a certain dollar amount in each category—say $5,000—helps me manage my workload and steadies my cash flow. If I only have a couple of thousand dollars' worth of work "on my desk," however, I need to get cracking on my efforts to line up more assignments. Otherwise, in another month or two, I'm going to be facing a dip in my income.

Try dividing your work into these three categories, and set a minimum dollar amount for each depending on your annual income goals. That way, when your "on-the-desk" work falls below that, you know it's time to beat the marketing drum.

Here are seven other techniques that will help create a more manageable workload and even out your cash flow:

ALWAYS MAKE TIME TO MARKET

To stay busy, you have to keep up with your marketing—being "too busy" is no excuse! You may find that rather than trying to do some marketing every day, it's easier to choose a specific time each week to work on pitching yourself and your business. Just make sure you stick to your "marketing day," even when you're swamped. Use this time to send queries and letters of introduction, e-mail follow-up letters, or reply to online posts looking for writers.

MAKE IT WORK

There are times when your work simply won't fit into the hours you've designated for it. That's one of the challenges of freelancing. Do what you can to meet your deadlines, whether that means working nights, weekends, or first thing in the morning. When I'm tight on time, I get creative about ways to cram some extra work into my day. I get up earlier (before my kids do!), put in an extra hour or so after they're in bed, and carry work with me so I can do some editing during my son's basketball practice. Think about what you can give up, at least in the short term, and "make it work," as fashion expert Tim Gunn would say.

AVOID THE PLANNING FALLACY

The planning fallacy refers to a proven fitness concept that people almost always underestimate the amount of time it will take to lose weight or get into shape. The same is true for freelancing—most writers think that assignments won't take as long as they wind up taking.

Break free from the planning fallacy by assuming that any project will take longer than you originally expect—and plan for that. For example, if you think a story will take a total of five days to research and write, plan for it to take seven. If you believe a book proposal will take you six weeks, plan for eight. It's better to have more time to finish a project than not enough.

START RIGHT AWAY

This is a corollary to the above tip. Too many writers take on assignments and don't get started on them until their deadline nears. Do the opposite—

as *soon* as you get an assignment, take the first steps you need to. For articles, that usually means doing background research and identifying potential sources. After I've come up with potential sources (whether experts or "real people" anecdotes), I start contacting them to line up interviews. I have to have my interviews done before I can write the piece.

CREATE A BUMPER

Here's something I didn't anticipate when I first started freelancing—how long it would take for me to get paid for an assignment. You can't control when work is assigned, or how long it takes an editor to approve it so you can actually get paid for it. For example, I pitched a piece to a magazine in May, which was assigned in July. I turned the story in in August, and in September, reworked the piece per my editor's specifications. After she accepted the story, she put payment through—and I received my check in early November.

Just as you assume work will take you longer than you expect to finish, you must assume that it will also take longer than you expect to get paid. That means you need to have a financial "bumper" to rely on when clients are slow to cut checks. Ideally you should have at least three months' worth of income in the bank; that way, you can withdraw from your "bumper" account when it's taking time to collect your receivables.

STAY ON TOP OF YOUR INVOICES

Just as you follow up on queries and letters of introduction, you should stay on top of your invoices. Note the payment cycles of your regular clients so you can check on invoices that remain unpaid once they're overdue. [See #67, Collect every check.]

HAVE A MIX OF EGGS

You've heard "don't put all your eggs in one basket." The same goes for your freelance work. It's easier to work for a small number of clients, but be careful about having too few projects going at any time. For example, last year I was counting on a book proposal selling so I didn't do much marketing. Then, when the book didn't sell, I suddenly found myself with little work—and little money.

I learned my lesson—now I always have a mix of work, no matter how busy I am. That way if I'm waiting for a go-ahead on an assignment or for an editor to approve a story so I can get paid, I have other projects to work on and less lost work time. It also makes me more productive because when I get tired of working on one project, I can switch gears and write something else.

Managing your workload and your cash flow isn't always easy as a freelancer. But planning ahead and staying on top of your assignments and your outstanding invoices will help ensure a steady stream of work—and checks.

BOOST YOUR VALUE

As a self-employed writer, your career is in your hands. No boss will suggest you learn Excel or take a class in book-proposal writing, if you've decided to make the jump from articles to books. But as a freelancer, you should set aside time and money each year for career development. As the publishing industry changes, the needs of your clients will change—and you must be able to address them.

Until 2010, I'd only worked with traditional book publishers. Then I decided to enter the world of POD, or print-on-demand publishing, to get a book I hadn't been able to sell into print. I spent several weeks learning about POD, its pros and cons, and evaluating possible companies before I chose CreateSpace to publish my book on ghostwriting. All of that research time was well-spent—now when I'm working with ghostwriting or co-authoring clients who are considering traditional and POD publishers, I feel comfortable advising them about the advantages and drawbacks of each.

"I think learning new skills helps differentiate you from writers who just write," says Boston-based freelancer Susan Johnston. "As journalism evolves, we need to evolve with it and that means learning how to crop photos, write SEO-friendly titles, and so on. Video is a great example of this. During Personal Pitch at ASJA this year, one editor asked me if I could shoot video to accompany articles. At first I hemmed and hawed, then miraculously, I remembered a video I'd saved on my iPhone and posted for my Facebook friends, which I showed her. I've been hearing about the growing popularity of video for a while and I've recently started experimenting with using video on my blog. I'm no expert but I now have a familiarity with the tools and how to use them."

That familiarity gives Johnston another skill to offer potential clients. She also suggests that freelancers consider learning how to format their articles in a content management system, or CMS, which more clients are requesting. Shooting and providing photos is another skill Johnston's editors often ask for, and she has learned to crop and resize photos to meet their specific size requirements. She's much more valuable than a freelancer who "only writes."

Lesson: You can't sit on your skills. Consider what kinds of skills clients or potential clients are asking for, and add more to your freelance repertoire. The more you can do for clients, the more likely they are to hire you—and turn to you with other kinds of projects.

81 MANAGE YOUR MONEY

By now you know the difference between a business and a hobby, and why it's important. According to the IRS, when you operate as the former, you can deduct expenses related to your business, reducing your overall tax liability. When you're merely a hobbyist, any dollar you make you from selling a product or service is taxable.

The IRS looks at a variety of factors when determining whether a venture is a business or a hobby, but the most important is whether you have a profit motive—in other words, your primary reason for writing is to make money. Then you must manage the money you're making.

At the minimum, that means:

SETTING INCOME GOALS. I don't care whether you freelance full- or part-time. You should have a specific income goal each year, whether you're a fledgling freelancer who would be thrilled to make $8,000 this year, or you've been at it a while and this is the year you want to crack six figures.

TRACKING YOUR INCOME. Setting an income goal is the first step, but you need to know how you're progressing toward that goal. Determining your "daily nut," or how much you need to average per day, will help you determine your progress. [See #71, Know your daily nut.] I'm always surprised when a freelancer says he doesn't know how he's doing financially. I can always tell you how much I've made so far at any point during the year, what my accounts receivable are, and whether they're overdue. You should be able to do so, too.

INVESTING WISELY. To freelance, you need basics like a computer, a website, Internet access, and a cell phone or landline. Just make sure when you spend money on your business, you're doing it for a purpose. I don't invest in new software or set aside money to attend a conference unless I've determined its value to me. Yes, you can write off legitimate business expenses, but you still have to pay for them! So be choosy about where you invest your money; the lower your business expenses are, the more money you make overall.

MAINTAINING A BUMPER. When I quit my job as a lawyer to freelance full-time, I had saved six months' worth of living expenses. That wasn't enough—my savings had dwindled to just over $100 before I started collecting checks on a regular basis. Get in the habit of setting aside a portion of every check, even it's just five percent of your money, to build your savings if you haven't already. Once you have six months of expenses set aside, set up a retirement plan.

SAVING FOR RETIREMENT. Self-employment means you're responsible for funding your own retirement as well. I netted less than $12,000 my first year as a full-time freelancer, but I opened an SEP, or simplified employee pension, with $1,000 before the end of the year. I aim to save 10 percent of my net income for retirement each year, but that's fluctuated depending on how much I've made and how much money I needed to contribute to our overall household income. With fifteen years in, I have about

$110,000 saved for retirement. I wish it were more, but I still have another twenty years of work to save, and will continue to contribute to my SEP until I retire.

As a self-employed person, you have several options to save for retirement, including an IRA, or Individual Retirement Account (either traditional or Roth); an SEP; a SIMPLE, or Savings Incentive Match Plan for Employees; or a 401(k) plan. Each has different requirements and limitations; check out the IRS' website (www.irs.gov), the Small Business Administration's website (www.sba.gov), or talk to your accountant about which plan is right for you.

PAYING QUARTERLY TAXES. When you're self-employed, you'll pay quarterly taxes, or quarterlies, which are based on your income for the prior year. Your federal and state quarterly returns are due January 15, April 15, June 15, and September 15 of each year. If it's your first year of freelancing, and you don't have a prior year's income to base your taxes on, set aside about one-quarter of your gross income to pay off your income tax at the end of the year. In the following years, you're expected to pay quarterlies on your prior year's income.

You say you'd rather write than worry about managing your money? Me too. But the way you handle your income may make the difference between success and failure in the long run. That makes it well worth your time.

PART 5
BALANCE: YOUR LIFE INSIDE AND OUTSIDE OF THE OFFICE

Yes, you're a freelancer, but you have a life, too (I hope!). Creating work/life balance, maintaining a positive outlook, nurturing your creativity, and staying physically and mentally healthy all have a tremendous impact on your productivity and long-term success as a freelancer. The secrets in this final section will help you avoid burnout, deal with writer's anxiety, juggle your freelancing with the rest of your life, and set the stage for a successful, happy life both in and out of your office.

82

BEAT BURNOUT

Freelancing full-time has a lot of perks. You get to make a living from your words, you can write from a home office in sweats and thick fluffy socks, and you can work as little or as much as you want. (At least you can in theory—sometimes you face freelance droughts or have to work weekends and nights to meet all your deadlines.)

Sure, there are the inevitable hassles with slow-to-respond editors, delayed checks, and mangled edits. But overall, most freelancers love what they do, and the way they're able to work. A survey of full-time freelancers I conducted in 2011 found that 90 percent "definitely" planned to continue their careers; another 7 percent said they "probably" would. So you may be surprised to find yourself suffering from burnout at some point.

With fifteen years of freelance experience (more than nine years full-time, the last six part-time), I'm far from immune to burnout. Instead, I can predict that every nine to eighteen months I'll go through a period where I seriously question my freelance career. Yet these times of burnout and self-doubt have helped me jump-start my enthusiasm for it and re-create my career. And you can do the same.

IDENTIFY THE BURNOUT SOURCE

First, you have to understand why you're feeling burned out before you can take steps to eradicate it. Do you have too much work overall—or simply too many deadlines that fall at the same time? Are your clients too demanding? Is it the type of work you're doing too demanding? Or is it that you're bogged down with "grunt work," things like transcribing interviews, chasing down money that's owed to you, or following up on queries you haven't had a response to?

Too much work at once can definitely cause burnout. But there may be other factors at play as well. Depending on your personal energy levels and personality, too little work can be just as debilitating. Several years ago, I went through a phase where I just couldn't muster any enthusiasm for freelancing—and I wasn't that busy. With too little work, I start to lose focus. I was in the middle of some major family drama (we were trying to adopt again and had a series of failed matches), and didn't have the time or mental energy to devote to my freelance career. It wasn't until I sat down and made a list of what was happening in my life that I realized why I didn't have any passion for my career. All of that energy was being shunted into handling my day-to-day life.

MAKE A LIST—AND CHECK IT TWICE

When you're feeling burned out, try my secret weapon. Sit down with your choice of caffeinated beverage and make a list of the pros and cons of freelancing. Look at this as a brainstorming exercise; don't worry about listing them in order of importance or how many you have on each side. Then read your list and compare the pros and cons.

The first time I did this exercise, I'd been freelancing for almost eighteen months. My "pros" list included thirteen items such as "no commute," "it's cool—I'm a writer," and "seeing my name in print." The cons included things like "I'm lonely," "continual rejection is affecting my self-esteem," "little or no feedback on work," and "no clear goals except for money."

Over years, my personal pros and cons list has changed, but some elements of my pros list have remained consistent. The freedom to set my own hours, the enjoyment of writing itself, and the fact that I'm building something that is mine are all reasons why I continue to freelance. On the cons side, I'm always frustrated about editors who are slow to respond or slow to pay (or worse, both), and I continually resent how much of my income goes to pay taxes. But on balance, is it worth it? Yes.

MIX UP YOUR WRITING

Seeing your personal pros and cons list in black and white should serve two purposes. Number one, it should get you excited about freelancing again. Second, it should give you insight into the parts of freelancing that aren't working right now. You can't do anything about what you pay to Uncle Sam, but if "bored silly by all my assignments" is on your list, you can start writing about a different subject area. Or maybe it's time to do something completely different.

Of course, if you freelance full-time or rely on your income to help support yourself and your family, you may not have as much freedom to explore other types of writing. Writing is your job, after all. But that can compel you to take on more work than you can realistically handle—and that definitely leads to burnout.

Strive for a balance of work and personal time, and spend time *away* from your desk. Working 24/7 may not kill you—but it will dampen your enthusiasm for writing full-time, and eventually you'll cringe at the sight of your computer screen. Time off is essential to freelancing success.

Recognize that burnout happens to everyone. It doesn't mean you can't hack it in a competitive business. Burnout is a symptom that indicates something should change. Whether you freelance fifty hours a week or five, you'll encounter it at some point in your career. Use it as a trigger to shake up your writing career for the better.

KEEP YOUR HAND IN

I was a full-time freelancer for more than eight years before I became a parent. I'd thought I'd been busy before—you know, with a husband, a thriving career, and a dog. Dogs are a lot of work, after all, so I figured I was prepared for parenthood. (You experienced parents can go ahead and laugh.)

In truth, I'd originally planned to take an extended hiatus from freelancing to be a full-time mom. But after about six weeks of nothing but baby/baby/baby, I had an epiphany. I wanted to work. I wanted to use my brain again. And I wanted a task that had a specific conclusion. (Any new parent will tell you that caring for a newborn is a seemingly endless cycle of feed/burp/change/repeat. And even when you're besotted by the most amazing little person ever created, it does get old.)

However, freelancing as a parent couldn't have looked more different than freelancing without kids. I could no longer spend all day at my desk or work when I felt like it. I had limited time, limited energy, and, I admit, limited patience. Ryan was my first priority and the only time I could be a freelancer was when he was napping.

After almost nine years of cranking out upwards of one hundred stories a year (plus books!), my productivity took a nosedive. The first two months of Ryan's life, I managed to research and write exactly *one* article—and even that took more effort than I expected. I decided to hire a part-time sitter who came to our house to watch Ryan. During the first month she worked, I researched and wrote two pieces. Progress!

I felt guilty about continuing to freelance after I had waited so long to become a mommy. But I missed coming up with ideas, researching stories, and pulling together something out of nothing. I missed talking with experts and editors. I missed making money. And I missed the deep satisfaction that writing—and getting paid for it—gives me.

I knew this wasn't the time to take on a complicated book proposal that meant weeks of research. But something was way better than nothing. So I focused on the small things I *could* do. I took on a few relatively simple stories, contacted reprint markets, and reached out to potential clients looking for speakers. I kept my business running, even if on a smaller scale.

Every minor task I did—researching a simple article on organic foods, selling a couple of reprints, lining up a speaking gig at a library—kept my freelance career alive. It also reminded me that while I was now a mommy, I was also still a small business owner with skills that have nothing to do with getting baby poop out of fat thigh folds. Each writing-related action helped me stay connected with my professional self.

By the time Ryan was six months old, I'd settled into a steady routine with my babysitter and knew I could count on working twenty hours/week. I accepted a book contract and multiple article assignments—and was soon making as much money as before he had come along. That was fortunate, as I had a new, unexpected expense—child care.

My point? There will be times when your personal life commands much or all of your attention, emotional energy, and time. Just make sure that you don't abandon the business you've spent months or years building. Keep your hand in and you'll find it easier to ramp back up when you *can* devote more time to freelancing.

STOP STRESSING OVER SMALL STUFF

I specialize in health-related subjects, which means that much of the work I do requires a lot of background research, including interviews with experts in their fields. That's usually a plus—I love talking to people and learning about new subjects. I've written about subjects as diverse as caffeine addiction, low-carb candies, sleep disorders, and massage, and I enjoy mastering a new topic.

But this kind of work necessitates spending a lot of time at my computer, locating and contacting potential sources, arranging interviews, conducting them, and then transcribing my notes. When I'm waiting to hear back from an important source—especially when I'm under a tight deadline—I'm pretty much chained to my desk. I like to tape and transcribe my interviews as I conduct them, and that's impossible with a cell phone.

The longer I wait to hear back from someone, the more annoyed I become. I'm annoyed that whomever I need to speak with isn't getting back in touch as quickly as I want him to (like, you know, this minute!). Then I start to worry. I worry that he won't return my call, and I'll have to locate a replacement source who's just as appropriate, or that I'll have to crank out a story at the last minute, or worse yet, that I'll run into deadline trouble. Once I start worrying, it's hard to stop.

But just as a watched pot never boils, a watched phone never seems to ring. So I don't hang around my office waiting for a call back from a source, especially when I've left my office and cell phone numbers, and told him what I need from him. I can't do anything but wait, but who says I have to wait at my desk? Sitting there won't force him to call me back more quickly, so I escape my office and distract myself by working at Caribou or running errands. And it never fails—just as I've forgotten about the person, he gets in touch. If he doesn't, I just try him again from wherever I am. That's the beauty of cell phones.

Early in my freelance career, I would have been too afraid to leave my office and miss a call. (This was before cell phones were as common as house keys.) But I've learned that sitting around waiting for something to happen doesn't make it happen any faster. It just makes me crabby and impatient. Now I do what I can (in this case, provide the source with all of my contact numbers) and try to let it go.

As a writer, you can count on being stressed at least part of the time. Some stress (worrying about doing a good job or making your deadline, for example) helps make you a successful freelancer. But if you want to write for a living, learn when to draw the line between worrying about the things you can't control as a writer and the things you can, and focus on the latter.

85

KEEP AN INSPIRATION FILE

Writing is a lonely business. By its nature it requires spending long stretches of time alone, and praise or even feedback on your work can be rare. Every writer needs a thick skin to succeed, but you can keep your motivation high during the lean times by keeping what I call an inspiration file.

An inspiration file is for your eyes only (unless you decide to share it with someone else). Mine includes a variety of notes, cards, letters, and e-mails that I've collected over the last fifteen years. In it is a handwritten letter from my mom, congratulating me after she read my first published magazine article. There's a card from one of my oldest friends celebrating my decision to freelance full-time, and a note from one of my editors thanking me for a job well done on one of my first stories. I even have "fan mail" from readers and notes from former students thanking me for helping them get published. When I'm having a bad day or feeling discouraged about my writing career (and believe me, it happens), I take a look through my inspiration file to focus on my accomplishments rather than on what's going wrong at the moment.

But I didn't start out with an inspiration file. When I first started sending out work for publication in college, I used to collect "bongs," or rejection letters. I taped them on the wall above my typewriter. (Yes, I'm that old.) To me, this was evidence that I was a "real" writer, and demonstrated my commitment even if I hadn't been published yet.

After collecting dozens of these letters throughout my twenties, I decided to toss them. I didn't need any help feeling discouraged. After selling my first articles to *Cosmopolitan* and *Bride's* and deciding to freelance full-time, I started a new collection of notes, which I eventually named my inspiration file.

Collecting positive notes is a much smarter approach than hanging onto the bongs you've gotten. Chances are that you're already your own harshest critic, so do you think that reading through rejections will somehow motivate you? I doubt it.

People are quicker to offer criticism or negativity than encouragement or praise. You probably already know that studies show that customers are much more likely to tell people about a negative experience than a positive one. That means the notes in your inspiration file may never outnumber the bongs you receive, and that's okay.

When you're struggling with your motivation to freelance, take a look through your inspiration file. It will remind you of the progress you've made and help reignite your enthusiasm for freelancing, regardless of how long you've been pursuing it.

JUST WRITE IT

In the last fifteen years, I've written close to a thousand query letters, more than eight hundred articles, a dozen book proposals, and thirteen books. I'm prolific (though not nearly as prolific as some other writers I know), so you'd think I never struggle with writer's anxiety. I only wish that were true.

The first few years of my career, I obsessed over every query and worried about every assignment. That's understandable—I had just launched my freelancing career and I was truly learning on the job. While I'd majored in writing in college, I had never taken a journalism class. I'd never written a roundup, a profile, or a sidebar. I'd never written a press release or ad copy or a brochure. Every time I tackled a new type of project, I'd read up on it and then figure out how to write the darn thing. Angst, anxiety, and fear ("Is this good enough?" "Will my editor realize I've never done this before?" "Am I kidding myself trying to freelance full-time?") were my constant companions.

But as I mastered different forms of writing, developed experience, and gained confidence, those worries dissipated. I knew what I was doing (at least I thought so) and I'd beaten writer's anxiety … until I started writing fiction again.

Working on my novel was creatively fulfilling and stretched my writing muscles in ways I'd forgotten about. It also filled me with constant, chronic dread. It's one thing to crank out service articles for magazines on easy ways to lose weight or how to boost your workout motivation or even what's new in birth control. But I was writing a *novel*. My novel. The one I'd tried (and failed) to write three times before. I wanted it to be good. No, I didn't just want it be good. I wanted it to be GREAT. Awesome. And, it goes without saying, publishable. All that pressure made me incredibly anxious.

Sure, I knew that all writers struggle with writer's anxiety at one time or another. I'd experienced it myself. But that fact didn't help me now. I was so worried that what I was writing was awful that my enthusiasm for my novel was leaching away. I needed a weapon to conquer my anxiety.

For me, the answer was to commit to daily fiction-writing time. That's how I churned out the draft of my first novel (and subsequent ones as well). I wrote a little bit every day. I didn't stop to worry about how bad it was (I obsessed about that the other twenty-three hours in the day anyway). Then, when I finished the draft, I printed it out and set it aside. I couldn't read it! I was that afraid it was horrible.

It took me two and half months before I could force myself to sit down with the manuscript. As I'd feared, parts of it were pretty bad. But lots of it was good, some small parts (dare I say?) great. I had some problems (like characters changing names three times, and forgetting to tie up some subplots), but nothing that was unfixable.

And I'd learned something. During my ten-week fiction-writing hiatus, I found I'd been just as worried and critical and angst prone about the novel as when I *wasn't* actually writing it. In fact, my anxiety had been worse. When I'd been engaged in actually writing it, that feeling lifted—even if only for a few minutes.

My point is simple. If you're struggling with writer's anxiety, stop obsessing over how bad what you're working on is ... and simply *write* the damn thing. It may be a temporary cure, but it works.

87

GET (AND STAY) PHYSICAL

What does it take to be a successful freelancer? Yes, you have to be able to write well, market yourself, develop relationships with clients, manage your time, and stay focused. You know that already. When I speak to would-be freelancers about making the transition from employee to business owner, though, I suggest that they commit to a regular exercise program—and look at it as part of their work time.

Writing is a sedentary job. And while using your brain is mentally draining, it requires little physical effort. I believe one of the reasons I've maintained a fairly high level of productivity (essential now that I freelance part-time) is that I've made working out a priority, even when I'm busy.

In my thirties, I ran five or six days a week. It was a great stress reliever until I started getting injured regularly. Now that I'm forty-something, I need a more balanced fitness routine. I still run, but not as often; I bike, lift weights, and do yoga. I try to make it to the gym four or five days a week, even when I'm busy. I know that after two or three days of nothing more physical than hauling my toddler around, my back gets stiff. I get cranky. I have trouble sleeping. I need the physical challenge and release of exercise to balance out the mental stress of work and life, so I make time for it.

Many of the most productive writers I know are dedicated athletes in some sense of the word. They run. They dance. They swim. They spin. They do yoga. They've figured out that a healthy body doesn't just look and feel good; it makes for a more productive brain, too.

As a freelancer, I need my brain. And I need to work. But it's all but impossible to shut that brain off. I'm always thinking about the assignments on my desk, encroaching deadlines, the amount of money I'm making, my plans for the next year, when I'm going to find time to write another novel, you name it. One of the rare times that I'm able to turn off the incessant mental chatter is when I'm standing on the pedals of a spin bike pushing through another two-minute sprint interval or trying to balance in triangle pose during yoga. Exercise that demands your full attention—I'm talking high-intensity, focused effort—shuts off your freelance brain, at least for a while. I need that.

A stroll around the block is better than nothing, but pushing yourself produces bigger benefits for your body and brain. Physical effort that causes discomfort also produces endorphins, which ease pain, decrease anxiety, and improve your mood. In other words, suffering (at least a small amount of it for a short period of time) is a good thing.

Rising to physical challenges makes you more able to handle mental challenges as well, and the reason is what researchers call self-efficacy. Studies prove that mastering physical skills (whether it's doing a headstand or successfully training to complete a 10k run) improves your self-efficacy, or your belief in your ability to perform a task. That self-efficacy bleeds into other areas as well, which means you'll be more confident, not only in your writing skills, but in your ability to weather an ever-changing freelance landscape and to continue to grow and develop as a self-employed businessperson. That's a sizable payoff for producing a little sweat on a regular basis.

Convinced yet? (Hey, remember I'm a personal trainer, too, so hopefully I've made the case for exercise.) If you already work out, you know all of this is true. If you don't, start. If you're worried about time away from your business, count your workout time as work time. The productivity and stress relief that result from a regular workout will more than make up for lost time at your desk.

88

WEAR A HAT

I make my living as a freelancer, writing primarily about health and wellness subjects. Focusing on these topics has helped me produce a good living despite radical changes in the publishing world over the last fifteen years, but that's not all I do. In addition to nonfiction, I write fiction as well.

And there's my challenge. The time I spend writing novels, which are by their nature "spec" work, may not translate into income. I can't count it toward my daily nut. As a result, I have to carve out time from my life to work on fiction, because I'm not willing to give up my limited work time to satisfy my creative needs.

The other issue is that I associate my office with, well, work. I feel guilty when I'm sitting at my desk and I'm not producing income, or at least pitching projects that may lead to income. To circumvent this problem, I invested in a portable word processor (an AlphaSmart I named Fred) to write the drafts of various novels in progress and do so anywhere but my office.

That's how I finished my first novel. Getting away from my office liberated me from worrying about paying work and productivity. But after my draft was finished, I had to sit at my computer to edit it. And I found it all but impossible. I was distracted with thoughts of paid work—articles, queries, nonfiction book proposals—the stuff I *should* be writing, not to mention the time I invest in selling books, updating my blog, and trying to maintain a social media presence. Fred had been great for the first draft, but now I needed something to create a division between my fiction (the work I do for love) and my nonfiction (the work I do for money) because I'd be working on both in the same physical space.

I thought back to college and had my answer. When I wrote fiction, I got into the mode by wearing my "Kurt Vonnegut hat." (*Breakfast of Champions* was my favorite novel and Vonnegut sported an old wrinkled hat on the photo on the back cover.) I'd bought my white terry-cloth fisherman's hat on sale at Kmart. I'd plop it on my head, drink coffee, smoke cigarettes (I know...yuck!), and pound out horrible short stories on my Smith Corona. If any of my two dozen roommates attempted to speak to me, I gave them a withering look and pointed to the hat. It meant I was not to be bothered.

My hat these days is blue canvas with a round rim, ventilation grommets, and a chin strap. It will win me no points with Tim Gunn, but I only wear it when I'm writing fiction. When I have my hat on, I don't check e-mail. I don't answer the phone. I don't log onto to Facebook or check my Amazon rankings. I don't think of new article ideas. I don't work on current assignments. I simply work on my novel.

My hat tells my itchy, distractible self that I'm writing fiction and fiction alone, at least for that small amount of time. If my husband asks me something, I yell, "Hat's on!" and ignore him—and I'm teaching my children the same rule. If I have to stop for some reason, to answer the phone or get the door, off comes the hat. When I'm finished with my fiction quota for the day, I take my hat off, where it will be waiting tomorrow.

If you're a writer like me who struggles with balancing work that you truly want to do along with the work you have to do, I suggest you use a physical reminder to give yourself permission to pursue the former. Like a favorite sweatshirt. A rope bracelet. Or a hat.

89

HAVE A BACKUP PLAN

I believe in planning my day. But often those plans go awry. Then what?

Say you get an urgent call from a client who needs edits on a piece you finished weeks ago—and he needs it today. Or you were supposed to conduct a critical interview for a profile you're writing, and now your source has gone AWOL. Or my favorite (not really)—you're a parent with a sick kid or a sick babysitter.

As a working parent, I've faced the sick kid/sick babysitter scenario multiple times—without missing a deadline. I may not have been quite as productive those days, but I've used multiple techniques to parent and work simultaneously. I have:

- Let my son watch as many episodes of *Blue's Clues, Dora the Explorer,* or *Top Gear* (depending on his age) as he wanted. A day or two of Ryan gazing open mouthed at the "magic box" isn't going to kill him.
- Allowed my toddler-aged daughter play with anything she wants. Unlike her brother, Haley isn't interested in TV. She loves, however, playing with anything she's not supposed to have. So I get out my office supplies (she loves padded envelopes), an outdated cell phone, an old remote control—anything that looks like it's forbidden and therefore fascinating—and let her go nuts. It's good for ten to fifteen minutes of work time before I have to find something else for her.

- Made the most of nap time. While it's a lot harder to entertain a toddler than an older kid, toddlers still nap. So, when she goes down, I use those precious ninety minutes to write as much as I can after a quick check of my e-mail. An encroaching deadline makes me write even faster.
- Gotten out of the house. Haley is still too young to run around the park without me keeping a close eye on her, but before she was born, I would take Ryan to the park or to a McDonald's playland and tune out the screaming children while I worked. As a member of the local Y, I have a free two-hour slot of babysitting time every day. I usually use the time to exercise; when I'm desperate, though, I bring my laptop and write instead.
- Called on a friend. When I'm truly desperate, I will call one of my fellow moms and ask to dump my kids on them for a few hours. This is a last resort, but I know I can if I must. (And I'm willing to return the favor. I can watch my friends' kids whether I'm working or not. Normally when I'm working, my sitter is here. So she does the child tending. Otherwise, I'm in mommy-mode anyway so a few additional children don't make any difference. Any mom of more than one child will tell you the same thing.)

Get the idea? Crises will arise, and the more children or family responsibilities you have, the more of them you'll encounter. Be a Boy Scout, and be prepared to make your day work however you can.

SAY "NOT RIGHT NOW"

Today, the majority of my work is ghostwriting and co-authoring books for clients in the health, fitness, nutrition, and wellness areas, but I didn't expect to become a ghostwriter. In fact, the first time I encountered the idea of collaborating, my knee-jerk reaction was "no way!" Turns out I was wrong.

It's been almost ten years since I first heard Sarah Wernick, Ph.D., speak about how she got started as a co-author. Wernick's first book, *Strong Wom-*

en Stay Young (with Miriam Nelson, M.D., a researcher at Tufts University), was a *New York Times* bestseller and launched her successful co-authoring/collaborating career.

During a panel at ASJA's annual writers conference, Wernick talked about how she identified potential clients, wrote book proposals, and then wrote the books with the experts after they sold to traditional publishers. She wrote one book a year and made a six-figure living.

I still remember sitting in the conference room and thinking, "Wow, she's making a lot of money!" Yet my next reaction was just as strong. I didn't want to spend a year of my life toiling away on *someone else's* book. No thanks.

So I wrote off the idea, pun intended, until years later, when I realized that if I wanted to keep writing books (and I did), I couldn't afford to spend so much time marketing and promoting them. I co-authored a successful book with Ellie Krieger, R.D., and got serious about collaborating with experts on *their* books. I also started ghostwriting.

So never say never. When I started freelancing full-time on January 1, 1997, I started my novel with a capital N. *The* novel. The novel I had dreamt of, fantasized about, and consoled myself with for years. I'd written short stories for years (none of which was ever published), but my goal had been to write a novel since I majored in rhetoric (writing) in college. And I got fourteen chapters down before I abandoned it. My next two attempts, novels that I started January 1, 1998, and January 1, 1999, also failed. I was crushed. I couldn't pursue my dream—I couldn't even *finish* a novel, let alone get it published. I was a failure.

I couldn't admit that to anyone for a long time. Finally I told one of my oldest friends, Abby, who I'd met in my first fiction-writing class. "I just can't write a novel," I told her.

Abby is a wise woman. She meditates, does yoga, and embraces a Zen approach to life, and she was quick to contradict me. "You just can't write a novel *right now.*"

It barely registered at the time, but she was right. Another year passed before I felt the urge to write fiction again. What was different this time? I wasn't just venting about my misspent years as an attorney (although once again my book featured an unhappy female lawyer). I felt more passion for this book, and I finished the first draft in four months, and the final draft in 364 days. (I'd given myself a year to write it.) That novel sold.

Imagine if Abby would have said, "Yeah, you're right," when I said I couldn't write a novel. Or, "What's the big deal? Most people can't." Or "I didn't think you could." Abby was right: I couldn't write a novel at the time. But I could—and I did—later.

So be careful what you say about your freelance career. And never say, "I can't," or even, "not for me," without adding "at least not right now."

91

SET FOOD RULES

When I started freelancing, one of my fears had nothing to do with making enough money or getting assignments from editors who had never heard of me or even how I'd survive as an extrovert, trapped working alone all day long. It was the fear ... of fat.

Like many women, I've struggled with body image and disordered eating. I gained more than fifty pounds my freshman year of college and struggled with bulimia off and on for a decade. While I overcame my eating disorder years ago, I retained some related habits, like eating out of boredom or anxiety instead of true physical hunger.

So you may be able to understand my concern about sitting at home with nothing to do but work—and potentially eat my way through my pantry. I knew I'd be anxious much of the time, and that I often used food to ease that anxiety. So, just as I had set specific goals for my business [See #72, Set both kinds of goals.], I set ground rules for working from home.

Those rules included:

- **EAT THREE MEALS (AND A MIDAFTERNOON SNACK) EVERY DAY.** I didn't want to fall into the habit of grazing all day long or to use food as an excuse for a work break. I sometimes would use lunch as a "carrot," though, promising myself an Amy's veggie burrito or a baked potato with cheese and fat-free yogurt (my favorite meal) if I met my morning goals.

- **AVOID SUGAR UNTIL AFTER DINNER.** Let's just say I have sugar issues. I've been known to eat entire bags of those fluorescent orange, chemical-laden circus peanuts. (I'm probably the only person keeping the company in business.) I know that if I eat sugar early on (even if it's an icing-laden cinnamon roll for breakfast), I wind up wanting to binge on candy all day. I can't live without M&Ms and jelly beans, but I don't eat them until after dinner.

- **WORK OUT EVERY WEEKDAY.** As a working parent with two little kids, this is a challenge. But remember, when I started freelancing full-time, it was just me, my live-in boyfriend (until he got smart and married me), and our dog. Sticking to my regular workout plan (usually a four- or five-mile run) Monday through Friday gave me an energy boost and helped alleviate some of the continual writer's anxiety I was experiencing. It also meant I didn't debate whether I would exercise each day—I only had to decide when I would exercise.

- **MAKE LUNCH A BREAK.** As a lawyer, I ate at my desk many days to save time. As a freelancer, I took a real lunch break every day. If the weather was nice, I'd take my lunch outside, or I'd watch a rerun of *Law & Order*—anything to give myself a mental break from work.

- **DRINK LOTS OF WATER.** I drank a can or two of Diet Mountain Dew every morning, but after that I switched to water. Keeping hydrated helped keep my energy high, filled me up, and forced me to take regular breaks away from the computer.

Sticking to these rules alleviated my worries about daily pig-outs and helped me stay physically and mentally fit even while I had my butt in a chair eight hours a day. I didn't gain any weight when I started freelancing, which was an accomplishment in itself. Fifteen years in, I'm not as strict with these rules, but I make time to work out as often as I can. And I still eat healthy most of the time, leaving room for my sugar habit.

If you've never had food issues, you may not need a set of rules like this, and if so, you're lucky. If you find yourself turning to food out of boredom or anxiety, though, I suggest you decide how and when you'll eat. Both your waistline and your productivity will benefit.

MAKE WAITING TIME WORK

In one of my favorite episodes of *The Simpsons*, "Mr. Plow," Homer decides to launch his own snow-shoveling business. With the help of singer Linda Ronstadt, he creates a television ad that runs in the wee morning hours (the only time slot he can afford.)

After the ad runs for the first time, he sits back and announces to his family, "Now we play the waiting game." But after only the briefest of pauses, Homer loses his patience. "The waiting game sucks," he declares. "Let's play Hungry Hungry Hippos."

Homer is so, so right. The waiting game truly does suck.

I know because I've played it before—and I'm playing it now. I have not one but four potential book projects that may or make not go forward. My agent is shopping around a book proposal I ghostwrote for a client. Another agent is shopping the updated version of a book I co-authored to its original publisher. A publisher has expressed interest in one of my own books but the editor has yet to send the contract. And another potential client is about to sign me to ghostwrite her proposal—any day.

So that means I have four potential book projects in the works, but nothing has signed yet. So I wait. And wait. And wait. Every time the phone rings or my e-mail chimes, I take a breath. This could be it! This could be the call! But it's not my agent or the AWOL editor or my potential client. It's another freelancer or a former student or a spammer. And I'm getting annoyed.

I know that something will shake loose, hopefully in the next few days. And I do have a few magazine articles to write, but not nearly enough work to keep me busy—or to keep me from staring at the phone, trying to compel it to ring.

So, what do I do in the meantime? I'm catching up on the things that always slip to the bottom of the to-do pile—like developing a promotion plan for the novels I recently published as e-books. I've pitched some new ideas in the hopes of getting more short-term assignments and touched base with former clients. I've caught up on e-mails, put up a bunch of new blog posts, and contacted a dozen of my reprint markets.

I'd be lying if I said I wasn't preoccupied about work, or rather the lack of it. But I know that although I can follow up, I can't force clients to sign. So I wait, and remember that in the freelancing world, it never rains. I just have to wait out the drought for the downpour—and hope I'm prepared for it.

If you're waiting on news of an assignment, especially a big one, it's normal to be distracted (and as my husband will tell you, cranky). But don't spend all of your time eyeballing the phone, checking your e-mail every five seconds, and listing all the reasons you're a loser.

Put your "empty" work time to good use by pitching new ideas, catching up on other projects, or improving your craft. The time will pass more quickly—and you may even forget what you're waiting for.

93

LISTEN FOR YOUR INNER VOICE

Ever had an epiphany? An unexpected flash of insight that teaches you something undeniably true? I've had at least a dozen in my life, including the moment I realized that law was the wrong profession for me (alas, only four days into my legal career.)

Yet not every epiphany announces itself with a bang. It may start with a still, small voice that's easy to ignore.

Years ago, I was working on my third novel, after selling my first two to a big NYC publisher. I'd sent the draft to my agent, who suggested well-founded revisions—the story needed more drama, more action, more heft.

I wrote pages and pages of notes about the characters and ways to improve the book, and finally sat down to begin the revisions. I wasn't having fun, but I'd already put nine months of work into this book. I found myself thinking, "I just need to lance this boil and get it over with."

About a week into the (hopefully) final revision, I was writing a letter to a friend when it hit me. Because I was quiet, I could hear that little voice. And it was saying, "I don't want to write this book."

There it was. The problem wasn't the characters or the plotline or the dialogue or theme or anything else. The problem was me. While I was fired up about the book when I started it a year ago, somewhere along the line, I lost the passion for it. (Comparing writing to lancing a boil is usually a bad sign, after all.)

Of course, my practical side tried to intervene. Was I really going to simply dump this book because I don't care about it anymore?

The answer is yes. I started writing fiction for the pleasure of it. I have plenty of work that I *have* to do, work that I get paid to write. That still, small voice—the one that always speaks the truth—proved that it was time to shelve this project. Better to go without writing fiction—at least for a while—than to force myself to work on something I don't care about, leaching the joy out of the creative process.

Shelving that manuscript wasn't what I planned, but it was the right thing. While it's important to be persistent as a writer, sometimes you do need to walk away from a project, to put your mistakes behind you and create some mental space and accessibility for the next project that you feel real passion for.

I'm learning to slow down and listen for that still, small voice. I hope you listen for yours.

PRACTICE DELIBERATELY

It's a widely held belief that simply doing a task over and over makes you better at it, and to some degree, this is true. But to really improve, you shouldn't just repeat it, you should be repeating it with some kind of goal in mind.

Let me give you an example. When I teach magazine writing, I have students write query letters. The day they bring them into class, they are afraid to share their work, and most of their queries are far from ready to submit. But as we critique them in class, they learn what the queries need: more details, a more thorough description of their approach to the piece, suggested sources that they plan to interview.

Their next set of query letters is always better than their first. It's not only because they're writing queries for the second time—it's because they're thinking about how to make them effective and how to make them appeal to an editor. That's more than writing; it's writing with a conscious goal in mind.

This type of writing is what Sage Cohen, author of *The Productive Writer*, calls "deliberate practice." The idea is that you just don't write and expect to improve; you write with a specific goal or set of goals in mind, and track your progress.

"Have you ever gotten halfway through a piece of writing and found yourself floundering about what you were actually trying to accomplish in the first place? This is where the concept of deliberate practice comes in," says Cohen. "When you set your sights on specific goals for a piece of writing, then you'll know exactly how close you come to achieving your goal."

Deliberate practice is "activity that's explicitly intended to improve performance, that reaches for objectives just beyond one's level of competence, provides feedback on results, and involves high levels of repetition," says Cohen. Athletes practice deliberately to improve their skills, whether it's a pitcher mastering a fastball or a gymnast striving for a perfect ten on the uneven parallel bars. Each time they practice, they (and often their coaches) are analyzing how well they're performing and looking for tiny adjustments that may make them even better.

To put this technique into practice, Cohen suggests that you "name and claim" the key objectives of every piece of writing you do. Here's her simple five-step process:

1. Choose a listener. In other words, whom are you writing this piece for? Write it down.
2. Name your objective. What goals are you trying to accomplish, and/or what goals does your client want you to accomplish? Write them down.
3. Write the piece.
4. Revise the piece, keeping your objectives in mind.
5. Evaluate the piece to see if it has met your objectives and the listener's needs.

"If you didn't hit the mark the first time, don't worry," says Cohen. "Remember, this is all practice. And the only way we improve is through repetition. Practice shapes us, so we can most effectively give shape to our writing."

I suggest you give Cohen's five-step process a try, especially if you're a new writer. Practicing deliberately will help you improve your work, regardless of what type of writing you do.

CREATE FREE TIME

I spent my forty-fifth birthday at an all-day CPR/first aid course I needed to take to maintain my ACE personal training certification. The class was scheduled on a Sunday, from 10 A.M. to 4:30 P.M., so I'd reminded my husband several times that he'd be watching the kids all day.

Well, my husband forgot. (Coincidentally he was studying for two IT certifications he needed to pass by the end of the month, so he was preoccupied. And crabby. When he learned he would be playing the role of dad, not IT student, all day on Sunday, he became even crabbier.)

But after opening my birthday cards and collecting extra kisses and hugs, I ran off for the class at my local Y. Lucky for me, we flew through the material and wound up getting out of the class about 3:15.

Did I rush right home to my loving husband to relieve him of our two darling but demanding children? Nope. Did I call him to check in? Nope. Instead, I took myself out for a late lunch (I'd had a bag of Cheetos during the class—not very satisfying fare) at one of my favorite little wine bars. (It was my birthday, remember?)

I tried two different pinot grigios and dined on an outstanding asparagus, goat cheese, pine nuts, and balsamic salad. While I was eating, the manager of the local running store (I'm a regular there) came in with her husband and I had a nice chat with both of them.

After a lovely hour, I got home just before 4:30 to an even crabbier, overwhelmed husband who thrust our toddler into my arms and ran upstairs to cram IT knowledge into his head.

And I didn't feel guilty at all.

Why not? Because I know how limited my "free" time is these days. And if I don't make an effort to create some, I never get any.

I was spoiled before I became a parent. I may have worked fifty-hour weeks to get my business off the ground, but I slept in on weekends, made social plans whenever I wanted, and didn't have to worry about the care and feeding of anyone but my dog and myself. (My husband has always been fairly self-sufficient and never expected me to cook. We survived on delivery pizza for years and neither of us minded.)

Then my son arrived, and four and half years later, my daughter. And that free time evaporated, though I need it more than before. So I'll tell you the truth. Sometimes when my sitter arrives, I leave so I can "work" at my local Caribou. But I don't work. I drink my nonfat latte and stare out the window. I think. I brainstorm. I fantasize. Or I just let myself sit, away from my desk, away from my office, and away from the two little people who call me Mommy.

I've noticed that most parents feel guilty when they take time for themselves. And that guilt is compounded when you're self-employed and taking time away from your business—not to mention paying your sitter $12/hour, even though you're not making any money right that minute.

But I've gotten over feeling guilty. I take some free time for myself every week, even if I have to pay for it—or take study time away from my husband. I'm worth it, I deserve it, and I enjoy every minute of it. You should, too.

96

FARM OUT YOUR KIDS

After eight years of full-time freelancing, my son arrived, changing my life and how I work. It took me a while to figure out how to blend parenting and writing [See #83, Keep your hand in], but one of the first things I realized was that I needed a baby-tender, stat! For me, trying to freelance and parent at the same time meant I did a rather poor job of each.

Yes, freelancing and parenting can be a great match. Unless you have children who are able to entertain, feed, and oversee themselves, however, you'll need some kind of child care arrangement. I'd rather pay for a sitter and use that time for focused, productive work than try to snatch five minutes here and there to run my business. For me, though, child care is a business expense, even if I can't write it off as one.

Ryan is now six years old and his sister, Haley, is nineteen months, and I've learned a lot about being a work-from-home parent since they came along. If you're making the transition to freelancing as a parent, or adding a child to your freelance life, keep these five strategies in mind:

Get real. I have friends who fall on both sides of the working/stay-at-home divide. I admit sometimes I fantasize about not having to worry about deadlines or making money or dealing with clients. I could "just" be a mom—a better mom than I am now, I'm sure. I could cook dinner from scratch every night, grow our own organic vegetables, start a compost heap. I could learn to sew and make our kids' clothes! I could homeschool our children and teach them Latin.

Then I'm jolted back to reality. The fact is, I dread making dinner every night, and I've never kept a houseplant alive for longer than a month. Even if I chose not to work, I wouldn't be knitting sweaters or grinding my own whole-grain flour; I'm just not wired that way.

I like working, and I want to keep on working, even with all the time challenges it presents. And I like that my work gives me a break from my kids. I'm not cut out to be a full-time stay-at-home-mom—and there's nothing wrong with that.

LIMIT VOLUNTEER WORK. To my clients, I'm a full-time freelancer. To the parents at school, I'm just another stay-at-home mom. Most don't know I work from home, but because I do, I can't be the "room mom" or sign up for every field trip or head up the PTA. But one of the reasons I work part-time is so I can be a more involved parent. So I volunteer, but I choose gigs that involve a shorter time commitment. I help with the school's semiannual book sale, volunteer for the YMCA's annual 5K/10K fund-raising run, and read at church instead of serving on time-consuming committees.

USE YOUR BRAIN. I lost out on a lucrative ghosting gig two years ago, and I'm sure I know why. I'd set Ryan up with a video and a snack so I could take a call from a potential client, and ten minutes in, he proceeded to have a monster, screaming meltdown. I apologized, but I could tell the potential client—a CFO at a Fortune 500 company—was anything but impressed. I should have scheduled the call when my sitter was there, but I wanted to talk to the person as soon as possible. That was a dumb mistake. It's better to push back a call than to come off as unprofessional, which is the impression I gave.

SACRIFICE SOMETHING. When you freelance and parent, you're going to have to give up something. I try not to let it be quality time with my kids. My mornings are devoted to running my business, but the rest of the time, I'm theirs. If I have to work extra hours to meet a deadline, I do that after they're both in bed. I would rather give up my precious "me time" than miss a trip to the park or the library.

EMBRACE YOUR CHOICE. I assumed that as a mom who works part-time, from home, I would avoid the working parent guilt thing. I was wrong. There are times that I have to check my e-mail or finish an assignment at the same time my son is desperate to play Monopoly or my daughter is trying to crawl into my lap, saying "Up! Up!" And I feel guilty. But my work helps support our family. It's important to me. And while I'm a mom first, I'm a freelancer, too. So I let the guilt go, or look for ways to avoid it in the first place.

I turned down a big book project two months ago because I would have to work forty-plus-hour weeks to meet the deadline. The money was excellent but I wasn't willing to put in the time, at least not right now. Another writer might have made a different choice, but I remind myself that my children will only be young once—and I have the rest of my life to run my business.

At the same time, I want my kids to understand that I have an identity that has nothing to do with them. I want them to see me as an independent, strong, capable business owner, not "only" a mom. For me, and for many freelancers, balancing both roles is the right choice to make.

97

CELEBRATE YOURSELF

Freelancing is a tough business, and compliments, acknowledgments, and positive strokes can be few and far between. That's why it's up to you to make the most of your achievements—and to celebrate yourself.

I've met few writers who are blessed with huge egos. Most of us tend to downplay our accomplishments, even to those closest to us. That's a mistake.

I was a full-time freelancer for more than four years before I felt ready to tackle a book. My first, *Ready, Aim, Specialize!*, was definitely the most challenging. I'd never written a book before and had no clue about what I was doing. I'd written hundreds of articles, but a book was another thing. I was compelled to overresearch, yet constantly worried that I'd leave something important out. I did dozens of interviews with experienced freelancers and researched hundreds of resources in the book.

My inexperience and anxiety meant that a book that should have been relatively easy to research and write became an overwhelming task. Oh, and did I forget to mention that during much of this time, I was freelancing for The Pampered Chef three days a week and keeping up with my regular article commitments?

I was stressed. During those months, I fantasized about becoming a best-selling author. Then I fantasized about seeing my book in print. Then I just fantasized about finishing the damn thing. I told my husband repeatedly that when I finished, I was splurging on a bottle of Dom Perignon to celebrate this momentous achievement. He'd nod, half listening.

Finally, after six months, I finished the book and mailed it to my editor. (This was before books were routinely submitted via e-mail, not the post office.) I called my husband and told him to meet me at our favorite restaurant to celebrate. When Erik arrived, he looked at me. "So? Are you going to order it?"

I balked. Practicality interfered with my fantasies.

"That's okay," I sighed. "It's stupid to spend the money. We can just get a bottle of something cheap."

Erik set me straight. "No way! You just finished your first book! We're getting Dom." He gestured at the bartender, who had to send a waiter to the basement to dig up a bottle. The bartender asked what the special occasion was, and soon all of the restaurant staff was congratulating me. That evening is one of my favorite freelance memories.

You may not always have someone around who will remind you that you're worth celebrating. Then it's up to you to fete your freelance achievements, whether it's finally seeing your work in a favorite publication, hitting ten thousand followers on Twitter, or selling your first books. Share your news with friends, family, and colleagues and bask in the glow of what you've accomplished. That glow doesn't last long (real life comes rushing back in before you know it), so embrace it while you can.

GET A PART-TIME JOB

I often say that I'm an extrovert with an introvert's career. One of my biggest struggles during my first few years of freelancing was dealing with the isolation the work requires. (Now that I have two young children, that's changed. I relish the chance to work alone!)

But it was my lack of social contact that led me to take a part-time job at Trader Joe's before I became a mom. "TJ's" is a hippie grocery store that sells everything from cheap wine like "Two-Buck Chuck" to fresh sushi to soy chips to gluten-free bread. After explaining my love for both human interaction and TJ's' meatless meatballs—and passing a math test—I started working ten to fifteen hours a week. I got my own neon Hawaiian shirt, a box cutter, and a nametag—something I hadn't had in more than a decade. Ten hours/week was just enough to give me some meaningful human encounters without jeopardizing freelancing.

The result? I got the contact I craved, built up my biceps (those wine boxes are heavy!), and found that many of my on-the-job lessons translated to my freelance career as well:

JUST DO IT. At Trader Joe's, I arrived, punched in, and got to work. One day I might be "pulling codes" (sorting outdated products), stocking canned soup, or breaking down pallets. Another day I might be working the register or working in the frozen foods section. But I never questioned whether I'd be working. I tackled the task given to me, finished it, and moved on to the next one. (Freelancing lesson: Don't gripe and moan. Just do your work.)

BE FRIENDLY. Trader Joe's is all about the unique products it sells—and the people who work there. As employees, we were expected to be friendly and approachable. Within a few weeks, I found I could start a conversation with any customer, any time—and people almost always responded positively. (Freelancing lesson: Clients like personable writers. So be nice.)

ANTICIPATE YOUR CUSTOMERS' NEEDS. At Trader Joe's, if you're wandering around open mouthed, scanning the shelves, an employee will ask if he can help you find something. (We're supposed to, it's in the employee manual.) In other words, you shouldn't have to track one of us down—we should be watching for you. (Freelancing lesson: Figure out what your client wants, and give it to her.)

ENTICE YOUR CUSTOMERS. Trader Joe's has full-time sign makers on staff to create eye-catching displays and decide which products should be displayed together. Put blue corn chips and black bean and corn salsa on the same shelf, and you sell more of both. (Freelancing lesson: Offer your client packages—say, a story and a sidebar, or an idea for a regular newsletter—and you'll get more work.)

Know your stuff. One of my favorite parts of working at Trader Joe's was recommending specific products to customers. I sold everything from peanut butter dog biscuits to yogurt-honey-peanut Balance Bars to low-fat soy chips. Being familiar with our products made me better equipped to market them. (Freelancing lesson: Be able to explain the benefits of hiring you to your clients.)

I may have only been making peanuts (and 10 percent off my groceries), but I loved working at Trader Joe's. The unexpected plus was that I became more productive with my freelance hours because I had to be. I could have worked there indefinitely but my manager kept overscheduling me and eventually I had to choose which was my priority—freelancing or TJ's. I chose the former.

Taking a part-time job doesn't mean you're not serious about freelancing. A job that you enjoy and that provides some of the things freelancing does not (human contact, structured hours) may make you recommit to your real job, that of a self-employed writer. If you're drawn to try something else part-time, at least for a while, I say go for it.

My Trader Joe's stint taught me a lot about freelancing. It also reminded me of how fortunate I am to have a career that I'm in charge of (not my surly manager), working the hours I want, from home, in pajamas—and with no need for a box cutter. That may have been the best freelancing lesson of all.

STAY FLEXIBLE

After fifteen years of running and multiple back injuries, I finally committed to something I'd said I *should* be doing for years. I signed up for a yoga class at my local Y. Long story short, I went to one class and gave it up.

Fast-forward another ten years and a few more injuries, and I again decided to try yoga. But not because I should—tell me I *should* do something and that pretty much guarantees that I won't. I'll resist, ignore, sidestep, you name it, but I won't actually do it. So what was different this time?

First, I was feeling older and stiffer by the day. Throw a twenty-pound baby into the mix, and it was a matter of time before I hurt my back permanently. And second, I took the class with a girlfriend. Grimacing and giggling at each other during poses made it a lot more bearable than going solo.

Eight months later, I can't say I love doing yoga. But I love having done yoga, and that's good enough for me. The classes challenge me in a way that running and lifting weights do not. I've learned I'm much weaker in some ways than I thought, but I'm getting stronger. I'm learning to push myself to the point of discomfort but not pain, and to become more present in the moment, at least during my sixty-minute class. Yoga has made me physically more flexible, and it's made me realize that flexibility is an overlooked but essential aspect of freelancing.

Staying flexible as a freelancer means:

ASSUMING THE WORST. I don't mean this literally. What I mean is to assume that things will go awry in your day, regardless of how organized and punctual you are. Case in point: When I call a source to conduct an interview, there's about a 25 percent chance that my source will ask me to reschedule or push back the time we talk. So I assume that, and plan for it. I try to give myself some breathing room and avoid scheduling interviews back-to-back and instead space them out in half-hour intervals.

CHANGING YOUR PLANS. This is a corollary to assuming the worst. I like to plan my day; I'm compulsive about making the most out of my time and a daily schedule helps me do that. But I will change those plans if I must. Say an editor e-mails with a rush rewrite request which she needs, well, yesterday. Flexibility means you have enough room in your schedule that you can attend it right away (or within the next day or two), and then get back to your other work. Responsiveness is one of the most valuable attributes you can offer your clients, and it requires a willingness to adjust your plans to address your clients' crises.

MODIFYING YOUR FOCUS. When I started freelancing, I could make a good living writing primarily for national magazines; I hit the six-figure mark with more than 80 percent of my income stemming from national magazine assignments. Things have changed. Magazines are smaller and are assigning shorter pieces, while competition among freelancers has skyrocketed. If I were still only writing for national magazines, I wouldn't be making anything close to what I was before, but I've segued into books, ghostwriting, and other kinds of work. Flexibility means branching into lucrative new directions, if necessary. What worked yesterday, or even two years ago, in terms of attracting and keeping clients, probably won't work today. That means you have to be willing to develop new skills and go after different types of work if necessary. [See #80, Boost your value.]

CUTTING BAIT. Being flexible as a freelancer also means not getting too attached to any one market, any one client, or any one type of work. The editor at your target publication didn't like your pitch? Query someone else. The agent of your dreams turned you down? Then he wasn't the right agent for you; try again. As a freelancer, you can't afford to only work for one client—what happens if that client folds, or fires you? Treat your clients well, do the best work you can, and keep your options open.

MAKING THINGS WORK. I've already quoted fashion guru Tim Gunn, but I'll say it again. *Make it work.* While writing this book, my computer started crashing. I backed up like crazy and made a mental note to plan on buying a new PC by year's end. After four unexplained crashes in an hour's time with four weeks to go before my deadline, I knew I had a problem. I used my portable word processor for a couple of days while my IT husband and I researched options. It cost two grand (my technology budget for the next two years) to get up and running with a Mac—but I was able to make my deadline and didn't have the stress of unexpected data losses.

Just as a rigid body will grow tight, a rigid approach to your day and your work will hamstring your success. Embrace a more flexible attitude and you'll find it easier to navigate your freelance career.

100

FIND YOUR OWN PATH

One of the most attractive aspects of freelancing is the freedom that it provides. Not only do you set your own hours, you decide how much you'll work, what kinds of work you'll perform, and what kinds of clients you'll work for. If you come to freelancing from a corporate job, that freedom is exhilarating.

It's also overwhelming.

Here's what I mean. Take a poll of a hundred freelancers, and you'll find that they're all pursuing different career paths. Deciding which one is right for you (often through a process of trial and multiple errors) can leave you constantly second-guessing your career arc.

I started out as a freelancer in a bubble. I didn't know any other writers, let alone any who worked for actual money. I was free to decide how to pursue my career without any role models to emulate or contradict. In the first few months, that meant working on my first novel and pitching (mostly poorly written) queries to national magazines. Then I started writing for the local paper and for local businesses. Then I decided to teach magazine writing at a local community college, which led to speaking at writers conferences and writing *about* writing. Then I started writing books. Then I started collaborating on books, which led to ghostwriting.

None of these things were in my plan. I didn't have a plan when I started out. I honestly didn't even have a clue. But I found my own path by asking first, what did I want to do, and second, what could I get paid to do? I still go through that process today.

My career looks very different than it did five or ten years ago. When I started out, I was a fledgling novelist, writing for magazines and newspapers to pay the bills. Five years later, I was a newly published author and successful magazine freelancer, balancing both roles. Another five years passed and I was a new ghostwriter/co-author who still kept her hand in with magazines. And now that another five years have gone by, I find that most of my work involves writing other people's books and doing motivational speaking on health and fitness topics. It's not the path that I expected but it's the right path for me.

Finding your own path doesn't mean that you ignore what other writers are doing or that you choose to follow the same trajectory of a successful freelancer. It means you observe, you pay attention, you gather information about what seems to be working for someone else and decide how you can apply that to your own life. You determine what appeals to you about the other person's work and what does not.

Take Jane Boursaw, the successful blogger who shares her advice in #77, Blog with purpose. She gets to watch movies—and get paid for it! I dreamt of being a movie reviewer as a new freelancer, mostly so I could impose my opinions on the general public. Boursaw makes good money as a blogger, which is also appealing to me. But you know what? She blogs all the time. That's critical to her success. She also has to watch movies she might not particularly enjoy, and she has to analyze those movies. She can't just sit and veg out in front of the latest romantic comedy; it's work for her. My point? No matter how appealing or attractive someone else's freelance career looks, I promise you there are drawbacks along with the plusses.

Yes, you should use other freelancers as guides. Just recognize that every writer's path is different. Don't blindly follow another writer up her path; pay attention to the unmarked trails that may offer you more promise and satisfaction. The path you take may not be the one you expected. But it will be yours.

101 SHOW UP ON YOUR MAT

When I go to yoga, the teacher tells us to honor ourselves for giving ourselves the time to practice yoga. We are reminded to honor ourselves for showing up.

There's an important freelance lesson in this. I guarantee that you will face obstacles as a freelancer. Stories will get killed. You'll lose clients. You'll deplete your savings. Editors will trash your work. Readers will post nasty reviews of your books on Amazon. Bad things happen even to good freelancers.

So I know at some point you'll question whether you want to keep freelancing. And maybe you'll decide to take a different approach. You'll decide to cut back on your hours, take a part-time job, go back to school, or take a vacation.

Or maybe you'll decide to give up on freelancing entirely.

About ten years ago, my husband and I hit the lowest part of our married life. We were experiencing infertility (which I wouldn't wish on anyone) and I wasn't sure whether our marriage would survive the stress and losses we were struggling with. And if I wasn't going to stay married, I didn't think I could continue to freelance. I'd need a day job again, health insurance, some sort of stability if I was going to be single. It was during this time that I flew out to Portland to speak at the Willamette Writers Conference and spend some time with my friend Polly.

We went for a drive through the hilly back roads of suburban Portland in her little 1995 Mazda Protégé. Polly managed to talk, steer, upshift, downshift, and take slurps from a giant cup without driving off the road while I clung to the passenger door. I told her what was happening at home and that I thought I was going to have to give up and get a real job. It was the first time I'd said it out loud.

She listened, and then she told me about her early freelancing days. While she'd planned for a successful transition from public relations employee to freelancer, during the first year her expenses outpaced her income and she was forced to borrow money from her dad to keep her business going. Her fiercely independent nature made this a low point for her—she hates asking anyone for help. But her dad loaned her the money and pointed out that nearly every new business needs capital early on. He told her he knew she'd pay him back—and she did.

A thought took form in my head. *I love freelancers.* And I do. I love the mind-set, the attitude, the independence, the intelligence, and the resilience that freelancers have. In that moment, I recommitted to freelancing. I decided to stick with it no matter what happened in my marriage, even if it was a lot scarier than the security of a job with health insurance and benefits.

That afternoon I got an e-mail from an editor replying to an LOI, which turned into steady work for the next nine months. I took that as a sign. I returned home with a new appreciation for freelancing. More importantly, Erik and I were able to work on our relationship and recommit to each other, and eventually became parents to the most amazing son and daughter in the world.

What changed during that adrenaline-producing drive? Nothing—except my attitude. I consciously chose to freelance. I committed. I showed up. That made the difference in my career and, I believe, in my marriage as well.

If you're struggling, don't give up.

Embrace your career choice. Claim yourself as a freelancer.

Show up on your mat.

INDEX